Contents

Foreword

They are never too young. The basic message of this bulletin is captured by this statement. According to Editor Alicia Pagano, "Social studies is a fundamental and essential subject area for teaching and learning in early childhood." For the most part, the social dimension of early childhood programs has been virtually ignored by social studies educators. Although children may encounter readiness experiences in mathematics and reading, preschools seldom give systematic attention to the social studies.

Challenging those who see socialization as a maturational process, Editor Pagano and her authors take the position that socialization must be skillfully and systematically guided by teachers who are well gounded in the social sciences.

The authors look at early childhood education through an interactionist lens. Young children both act upon and are acted upon by the environment. The teacher's task is to create stimulating learning settings and experiences with which children can interact. This interactionist perspective is reflected in each chapter, giving the bulletin internal consistency.

The authors are knowledgeable and experienced persons in the early childhood/social studies fields. Their efforts represent the first time that a major NCSS publication has addressed the concerns of early childhood. We are most appreciative for their contributions and commitment.

Anna S. Ochoa, *President*
National Council for the Social Studies

Social Studies in Early Childhood: An Interactionist Point of View

Alicia L. Pagano, Editor

National Council for the Social Studies · Bulletin 58

NATIONAL COUNCIL FOR THE SOCIAL STUDIES

About the Editor

A specialist in early childhood education, **Alicia L. Pagano** has taught in child development programs in elementary schools and in preservice teacher education programs at the university level. She has served on the faculties at William Paterson College in New Jersey, Montclair State College in New Jersey, and the University of the District of Columbia. At the present time she is Assistant Professor of Education at the City University of New York.

The author of publications on childhood education and organizational management, Dr. Pagano is Vice President of the Early Childhood Division of the Metropolitan Association for Childhood Education, an affiliate of the Association for Childhood Education International, and a member of the NCSS Early Childhood Committee.

Chapter Authors

Loren Weybright, Director of Research in the Day Care Training Program, School of Education at the City University of New York

Lois Wolf, Director of Special Projects, Graduate Faculty at Bank Street College of Education, New York City

Nancy Wyner, Assistant Professor of Education at Wheelock College, Boston

Carol Cartwright, Associate Professor of Early Childhood Education, Division of Curriculum and Instruction at Pennsylvania State University at University Park

Luberta Mays, Assistant Professor and Chairperson of the Division of Teacher Education at Medgar Evers College of the City University of New York

Library of Congress Catalog Card Number: 78-57997
ISBN 0-87986-022-7
Copyright © 1978 by the
NATIONAL COUNCIL FOR THE SOCIAL STUDIES
2030 M Street, N.W., Washington, D.C. 20036

Introduction

Young children are always busy! Try following a child through a day and see if you can keep up. Look at the photo essays on the following pages and you will observe children. They hang from jungle gym equipment, swing back and forth on top of tire swings, or just walk through the woods alone. What are children doing when they are engaged in these solitary activities? How may these behaviors illustrate their growth and development?

Children crawl under boxes and play "pig" or "dog" or "rabbit." They chug their trucks over child-made bridges and they become truck, truckdriver, and oncoming traffic all in one. What imaginations! How do these behaviors contribute to cognitive or social development? Will these fantasies help children learn to read and to get along with others?

As classroom teachers, you are observing children each day so that you can plan quality learning environments for them. These varied actions of children in their own physical world and their interactions with people are important. These are the ways children learn. These are the ways children build cognitive structures for understanding the social symbols of our society and for becoming effective citizens of the world.

In the following chapters of this book, we will present an approach to early childhood education which places *social studies* at the center of the curriculum. This approach combines two important ingredients: (1) the development of the child within society, and (2) the subject matter of the social science disciplines as expressed in social studies. Development will be viewed from an *interactionist* perspective which recognizes the child as an active participant in personal learning. It is hoped that this combination of ideas, as expressed by the several authors, will be helpful to you in your daily experiences with children in the classroom and in your long-range views about social studies in early education.

Alicia L. Pagano, *Editor*

The three Photographic Series that follow focus on children growing and developing through action and interaction.

Photographic Series One

Action upon the Physical World

Photographic Series Two

Social Interactions:
Integration of Social and Cognitive Development

Photographic Series Three

Teacher Observation Techniques:
Observing the Moment of Learning

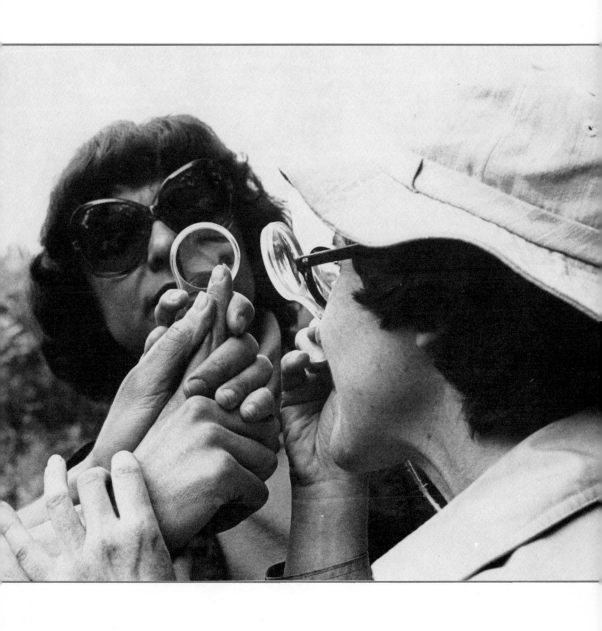

1
Young Children Growing Through Action

Loren Weybright

Children are active, as you have noticed from the photo essays on the previous pages and as you observe them in your classrooms each day. They are always on the move and they are always in the process of growing and changing and learning. They are learning how the world works and how to get along with themselves and with others in this world.

One of the most difficult tasks for the classroom teacher is to support the growth of children with a curriculum that is meaningful to them in the context of society. This chapter illustrates how the developmental approach provides a framework for a curriculum to guide young children in their investigations of their social and physical world. It places *social studies* at the center of early childhood education.

Historically, the integration of developmental theory and pedagogy is found in:

1. the growth of the kindergarten and nursery school movements, with a focus on socialization,[1]
2. the progressive education movement, with its emphasis on the active involvement of the learner,[2]
3. the social studies curriculum reforms,[3] and
4. the open/informal education movement.[4]

Presenting a developmental point of view of social studies education for young children suggests the importance of a statement by O. W. Markley: "A central function of all social institutions becomes that of human development and self-regulation, rather than of fostering bureaucratic efficiency and centralized influence."[5] It would follow, then, that a primary role of the school would be to support children's gradual development and self-regulation.

The practical and theoretical implications of developmental education focus on four themes. These themes are:

1. Growth through *action and interaction*, focusing on children's and adults' active involvement in their own learning.
2. Growth within the *developmental stages*, exploring the strengths of the different levels of development during the early childhood years of three to nine.
3. Growth through *integration*, supporting the natural connections between social and cognitive development, and between moral and logical actions.
4. Growth, as recorded by *observation* of children, objectively documenting continuities and changes in children's behavior over time, relating the development of children's ideas with plans for children's actions (i.e., curriculum), and connecting practice and theory.

Action and Interaction

The central idea that growth occurs directly through action and interaction is reflected in ordinary observations of children or adults. Children, when confronted with something new, quite naturally approach the object or event by feeling,

.smelling, tasting, probing, or watching. As Hawkins recommends, we might best explore new things by first just "messing about" with all our senses and actions.[6]

Action and Interaction Support Growth

The concept that children's action and interaction support their growth is described in developmental theory and is observable in the lives of growing children. The origins of logical thought and social cooperation are based on children's actions. These actions include the visible, external actions as well as the internal actions. Young children's *external* actions are readily observable while they are in the active process of discovering how to construct a block tower or of learning how to share objects and ideas. The *internal* organization of actions or ideas, such as comparing leaves collected on a walk, counting blocks, or learning social roles in a dramatic play, can only be inferred from visual observations or from records of children's overt actions and explanations.

Development occurs as new actions are integrated into the current understanding of the child. The integration of internal and external actions appears early in infancy. Infants' first actions are external, sensory and motor investigations of things or people. These early actions serve to develop, later, internal ideas about the permanent nature of objects and of people. For example, in the *physical* realm, infants only gradually retain the idea of a "rattle" as an object that has permanent identity. At first they grab it, shake it, taste it, and generally explore the object "rattle" with external actions. Once the rattle disappears, they seem to forget it. They immediately lose interest and become involved with something else. It is as if a rattle can be real one moment and then not exist the next moment. The permanent, internal idea of "rattle" does not come about merely by adults *showing* the passive infant that the rattle is still there but just out of sight. Permanence of an object cannot be taught. Infants must physically "mess about" with objects over a period of time as they gradually begin to construct an internal idea about the physical world—about that rattle. Ideas about all other objects or persons are formed in this manner.

The development of children's permanent ideas about the "roles" people acquire in real life is an important example in the realm of *social* action and interaction. As young children act out the roles of mothers and fathers, or of police officers or teachers, in dramatic play, they begin to define, and eventually to internalize, the meaning of these roles for themselves. Initially, these roles have a private, one-dimensional meaning. This is one step along the way to the development of role concept. At this early stage, children in dramatic play often insist that there is only one way to be a "mother"—*their* way. When a single role for mother first becomes defined, it is difficult to generalize to a dual role and to imagine that a mother can also be a doctor or a scientist.

The gradual definition of role, single or multidimensional, is actively explored in the following example of dramatic play. Several six- and seven-year-old girls were trying to decide who would play which role in a family setting. When an inpasse was reached they tried to use a choosing game, but no one was able to make it work. Note how the girl S appears to conclude that a person could have two roles at the same time.

> T: I'm the sister.
> C: I'm the mommy.
> T: I want to be the mommy. You're always the mommy.
> C: OK. You be the mommy.
> S: One of you could be the grandma.

(The conversation goes on; they try the choosing game; finally A proposes:)

> A: I know. You (T) can be the baby and you (C) can be the pet sister.
> C: Wait. Why don't we all be neighbors?
> T: No, all the cousins are coming over.
> A: Hey, she (C) could be my sister.
> S: That means she's a cousin and a sister.

(They do not come to any conclusions until C starts the role-play by announcing:)

> C: (To A) We're babies.

(They play patty-cake; then try to crawl out of the area when T stops them.)

> T: I'm keeping an eye on you!

In the end, the differences in their individual choice of roles were resolved by taking a new

role in which they could both participate—crawling about as babies.

It is significant, for both pedagogical and developmental reasons, that the girls in the above example kept trying to look beyond their own choices for solutions to their role-selection problem. They tried an objective choosing game and were willing, when challenged, to relinquish a chosen role. Rather than persist in their individually selected roles, they looked for a solution satisfactory to the group as a whole. The problem was solved through action.

Adults who support role-playing activities create a familiar, active setting for further development with other social science concepts, such as solving problems with alternative solutions and arriving at decisions framed outside of one's own viewpoint. (Additional specific situations involving problem-solving and decision-making are presented in Chapter Two.)

Implications for Social Studies

Lucy Sprague Mitchell, in her book *Young Geographers*, outlines a methodology that is active for both the teacher and the students.[7] Although this work was written in the 1930s, it has current applications and is still considered innovative.

According to Mitchell, there are two phases of the learning process. The first phase is when people gain information through inquiry, exploration, and observation of their own environment. The second phase occurs when they seek relationships in this environment and integrate the new information into their current knowledge. This method of learning requires action on the part of the learner. Mitchell outlines the role of the teacher as follows:

1. The teacher explores the environment to develop a practical sense of the community that surrounds the school. In a way, the teacher personally becomes a "geographer."

2. The teacher observes children in order to understand their ideas and actions and to gain their point of view. This is done to plan teaching situations in which the children can become "young geographers." These situations are:
   a. Planning trips into the surrounding community so children will be able to make firsthand observations and will use the environment as a laboratory.
   b. Providing classroom environments where children can return and relive their experiences, work out relationships, and integrate their observations.

If teachers are going to help children discover the world in which they live, the teachers themselves must first understand the functioning of this world. They can do this by going out into the neighborhood to observe, investigate, collect data, and come to some conclusions about the particular character of the community. They will talk with the residents and shopkeepers and interview people who provide the basic services to the community. They will look for the answers to many questions, such as: How do stores receive their fresh vegetables? Where do people earn their living? Who repairs the cars? Is there public transportation? Who uses the river? Are there older people who would be interested in sharing a skill or oral history with the children? What is special about this community? These are just a few questions. In moving through the geographic areas of the community, teachers would begin to acquire a practical knowledge of the neighborhood. They would note the human geography, as well as the physical geography of the area. They would extend their own understanding of its functions and would record how the community could become a laboratory for the children's investigations.

Teachers and other adults were also encouraged by Mitchell to observe children so they could better understand the children's point of view. When adults provide different opportunities for children to represent their recent experiences through dramatic play, art, or with blocks, the children quite naturally reveal their understanding of the social and physical world. For instance, following a trip to a local market, the teachers would be able to recognize the children's impressions of stores and storekeepers as these ideas were reflected in their block play or in their drawings. The teacher could then ask appropriate questions to stimulate the children's thinking. Samples of children's work, their repre-

sentations of reality, provide important sources for observing and documenting their growth. Techniques for observations of children's actions will be further discussed later in this chapter.

The learning activities for the *children* are also based on a social studies curriculum of firsthand experiences. These activities follow through from the environments planned by the teachers (see previous outline on teacher's tasks, 2a and 2b). The phrase "young geographers" implies that the children themselves may become the explorers, testing out their ideas. The children, in order to understand the different people and their roles in the life of the community, will need to go out and observe and interact with people in the most direct ways possible. For example, several children and an adult could examine some aspect of their daily lives in a detailed manner. A visit to the local laundramat to observe how it is used, where to put the money, where the water comes from, what happens inside the machines, how long it takes, who comes in to use the machines, and who keeps the center clean would pro-

vide new information about a service already familiar to many children.

The second task for children is to represent actively the images they have created through their direct contacts with the larger community. They may want to use clay to build a washing machine or paint a picture showing clothes tumbling in the drier. Adaptable, unstructured materials are recommended for this activity because these materials provide greater freedom of imagination and use of the children's own ingenuity. The multiple functions of unit blocks, cardboard boxes, clay, or water paints would give individual children an opportunity to express their experiences more adequately than would the less flexible commercial toys.

The same types of exploration in the community could be accomplished within the environment of the school itself. The teachers could examine the building with a different approach to determine new relationships. For example, they might observe something as simple as where the steam pipes in the classroom come from and where they lead.

Exciting new discoveries can be the out-

growth of this approach. For example, in the Lefferts Park Elementary School in Brooklyn, a construction worker discovered in the basement a brick arched doorway that led to a previously concealed storage room.[8] This discovery captured the children's imagination. They began to explore the construction of the school, when it was built, and who the workers were who built the structure. Children talked with people in the community and learned about the craftsmanship of the Italian immigrant bricklayers who had worked on this construction. They discovered that some of their own relatives had helped to construct their school. As the children brought this information back to the classroom, they made drawings of the workers and collected photos of the community and school. The project culminated in a week-long festival where people came in from the community to demonstrate Italian-American crafts to the children. They made spaghetti, wood carving, embroidery, and leather work. Children joined in to make their own crafts for display. Through these experiences, the whole community benefited. Foreign-born parents no longer felt alienated from the school, and both parents and children gained in self-image and a sense of belonging. There's no graffiti or vandalism in this school! (For the importance of parent involvement, see Chapter Four).

Children can also learn *mapping* through their actions and interactions in the environment. Mapping, as another form of representation of the real world, often begins quite spontaneously in children's block play, as they arrange their roads and buildings and open spaces in the ways they imagine them to be. Large school blocks and boxes in the classroom encourage children to play the roles of people in the community and to express representations of physical space with which they are familiar. From the children's geographical understanding of a recent trip around an island, they may construct their own island of blocks on the classroom floor, get in their boat, and sail around the structure. Through action and interaction with materials and with themselves, the children then begin to develop a "muscle image" of an island. This physical feeling will help children understand "visual images" of places they have not visited.[9]

Need for Personal Connections

Children need a close relationship between the content of their investigations and the social studies content of the curriculum. They require personal connections with their explorations of the past or present and in their examinations of the physical and social world. (For a personal definition of each of the social studies content areas, see Chapter Six). Dewey points out that the social sciences should be presented in direct relationship to the daily life of the students' social groups, rather than as preformed bodies of knowledge.[10] Weber and Osborne also propose that if teachers account for children's personal relationship to the subject matter, social studies is inevitably built into the curriculum at all stages of children's development.[11]

Children bring many different views to the classroom that are based on the circumstances of their family, their ethnicity, and their particular community. The teacher's primary role is to encourage the expression of these special meanings in their classrooms.

The relationship between external and internal actions found in all forms of representation is a strong one. The external actions of young children, as they play with objects in the physical world and as they socialize with their peers in their social world, support and extend the internal mental actions. The internal actions of thought develop gradually as young children learn to represent various roles, and, more generally, learn to symbolize their ideas about their world. The theme of action and interaction appears as both an internal and external process. It flourishes in both physical and social contexts and occurs across all ages.

Developmental Stages

The second theme which supports the connection between development and social studies is that of developmental stages. This theme:

1. identifies the essential actions or "stages" which distinguish children's thinking from adults' thinking, and
2. describes similar processes of change occurring across and between stages.

Psychologists have shown that, contrary to what was once assumed, children not only know less than adults but that there are fundamental differences in the form and the pattern of thought, roughly defined according to age. These patterns of children's ideas about their physical and social world differ in fundamental and often dramatic ways from adults' ideas. A preschooler, for example, called to his father, "Get behind me, Daddy. Then they can't see you." Another child proclaimed, "I have feet. You have feet. Curtis don't have feet. He's not here." From young children's points of view, everyone sees just what they themselves see, and nothing else.

While the first theme of *action* in this chapter described *processes* found among all ages, the second theme of *stage* draws upon the qualitative differences in the *content* of children's actions within and between stages, and their corresponding ages.

Preoperational Stage

The relevant stages for the early years are found in Piaget's descriptions of the preoperational and the concrete operational stages.[12] While the preoperational stage is often discussed in terms of what it lacks in comparison with adult thinking, teachers can direct attention to the strengths of young children to provide the basis for planning a social studies curriculum that is designed to reflect individual children's current and evolving developmental levels. Preoperational children may be partially characterized by their strengths. These strengths include:

1. their growing ability to represent their world through symbols and signs,
2. their beginnings at separating objects or events from their names or symbols, and
3. their developing languages of actions and words.

The preoperational stage begins with the development of symbolic thinking. Young children represent their ideas, their meanings, and their symbols about objects or events through language, imaginative play, physical action (counting or sorting objects), and social interaction (role play, friendships, sharing). Piaget and Vygotsky suggest that

young children's understanding of the relationship between objects and the objects' meanings or symbols develops out of their social interaction with peers and adults.[13] This is one reason why the social studies curriculum, with its emphasis on social interaction, is important in the early years. The object/symbol relationships found in young children's actions are essential to all later development. They are necessary for children's growth in social studies, in reading, and in mathematics.

At an early stage of symbolic thinking, the symbol appears to be fused with the object it represents. Perhaps this is why young children have a natural interest in the use and the origin of names. For example, Piaget recorded the spontaneous remarks of two children (six and one-half years old) during their play with building blocks.

> One child remarked, "And when there weren't any names . . ." The other child replied, "If there weren't any words it would be very awkward. You could not make any thing. How could things have been made?[14]

The implication was that if there were no names, the objects themselves would not exist. The name of things, at this stage, appears to be the essence of things.

As preoperational children begin to build the framework for truly logical or operational thought, several limitations are evident in their actions. These children are often egocentric, centering or narrowly focusing on their own views. They recognize, for example, only a single dimension of a social role at a time, believing that teachers cannot also be mothers or fathers. They depend extensively on concrete, firsthand sensory and motor actions, making their thinking somewhat rigid and immobile. Teachers of young children who understand both the strengths and the relative limitations of this stage can provide optimal learning environments and opportunities that give the children experiences to grow within this stage and into the next sequential stage.

Concrete Operations

Concrete operational children can be characterized by their growth out of egocentrism toward social cooperation. They are able to "decenter," to move to a view where self is not the only concern. They no longer focus completely on their own view, but begin to understand the validity of another perspective. In terms of specific logical actions or "operations" in the physical world, they are able to arrange items from the largest to the smallest, ordering and serializing objects and events. They begin to "conserve," or to hold constant, several properties of an object at once. This frees them to conserve the multiple properties of the physical world: to understand such concepts and relationships as time, space, matter or weight.

They also learn to classify objects or people into groups and subgroups. While concrete operational children are able to classify, order, and serialize objects or people, they remain confined to raw, perceptual data. Children at this level are able to operate on real objects, but they are unable to test hypotheses on data which are not directly observable. Abstract hypothesis testing and thinking about thinking are not attained until the formal operational stage of adolescence and adulthood.

While conserving and classifying characterize the entire period of concrete operations, it is the children's ability to classify people, events or objects that has direct implications for the social studies educator. The teaching strategies recently developed in several of the social studies curriculum projects have emphasized the development of classification skills. Such programs include those by Taba, Bruner, and Sigel.[15]

Adults who work with young children will better understand the acquisition of classification operations through a knowledge of current techniques in interviewing. Two methods are:

1. administering the standard Piagetian interviews, and
2. recording children's actions and conversations during their ordinary, daily investigations of their physical and social world.

As teachers collect a variety of examples of children's classification activities, they will begin to observe common patterns that indicate developmental levels of particular children. Collecting evidence of logical thought as it occurs in ordinary play settings draws attention to the organic relationship between these natural actions of children and the development of thinking itself.

The following example of children's spontaneous use of classification action was recorded with a group of five- and six-year-old boys during their block play. The boys had been playing "cops and robbers" for some time when R picked up a toy dog and began to bounce it around, howling. The observer asked him what it was:

    R: That's a police wolf.
    T: (Looking at the observer) There's such a thing as a police *wolf*?
    S: It's a police dog.
    R: No, it's a robber dog.

(They play a bit more. R continues to bounce his wolf/dog around the block area.)

    R: (To himself) And the dog couldn't find nothing to eat ... And then they put the robber in the jail.

(He throws the dog into their block "jail." D now has a giraffe, and he begins to follow R's wolf/dog).

    T: Get that! (Disgustedly) We don't have no giraffes!
    A: Just a wolf.
    T: That's a police wolf. We don't play with animals and cops.
    A: But wolves are animals.
    T: But they ain't reptiles.
    A: I know that. People are animals.
    T: But dinosaurs are reptiles.
    A: But people are animals, not reptiles.
    T: Why? They don't have no tails ... 'cause they bite?

(No answer. The activity goes back to wheeling cars and capturing robbers.)

The external actions observed, and the internal processes inferred in the boys' discussions about police, people, wolves, and other animals, reflect their growing understanding of classes and groupings. Their conversation also reveals the application of classification in a social context; that is, the children's developing sense of what behavior was appropriate for which role.

Implications for Social Studies

The characteristics of each developmental stage provide common guidelines for those who work with young children in the social studies. Piaget identifies the basic human qualities which support growth and movement within or between stages as:

1. being open to and ready for change,
2. being active in exploring and examining the environment,
3. being self-regulating by striving for equilibrium or balance—a balance between consolidating new patterns of thought and changing old patterns of understanding.[16]

Based on observation and understanding of children's ideas, teachers support growth through meaningful, adaptable materials and activities which encourage the active involvement of the learner.

Acknowledging the existence of stage and sequence of development does not imply, however, that growth through the stages should be accelerated. Rather, those who work with children are encouraged first to carefully observe and record children's ideas in action; then to examine the collected ideas for larger themes that more accurately describe a particular child. While stage classification helps us to understand children's behavior and level of thinking, these classifications should not be used as mere labels for a child's intellectual and social progress. Observations of the total context of a child's behavior, which may include stage considerations, provide teachers with a framework for supporting that child's development in general, and furnish beginning points for growth in specific social skills.

Integration

The third theme describes the integration of the development of logical thought and children's ideas about *rules* and *moral judgments*. Play and social interaction provide a natural setting for the development of social thought and moral action, behaviors that are central to social studies education. Both Piaget and Vygotsky propose that the voluntary constraint of rules in play support the development of social cooperation, cooperation which characterizes the development of both logical thought and moral judgments.[17]

Cognitive and social development during the early years are described by Piaget as the growth from egocentrism and natural constraint towards the development of social cooperation.[18] The stages involved are described as the two moralities of childhood. They are:

1. the morality of adult constraint, and
2. the morality of social cooperation.

Constraint and Egocentrism (Preoperational Stage)

Children's judgments, in the morality of constraint, appear to be held back by the external rules of adult authority. Once children learn what a rule is, they believe it can't be changed. The rule was made by an adult; only an adult can change it. Children adapt to the natural adult authority by placing rules on the level of moral absolutes; i.e., judging wrongdoing on the basis of external evidence, not internal motives. For example, young children feel that someone who knocked down many blocks by accident should receive more punishment than someone who knocked down only a few blocks, regardless of motive.

The informal rules or procedures that children use to portray roles in dramatic play are often characterized by an inconsistency between awareness and practice. The children may claim that the rules for their play are sacred; but, unwittingly, they often ignore their own rules in practice. The following discussion about rules was based on observations of five-year-olds in dramatic play. In this situation, few rules were spontaneously declared, and most were elicited by the observer's questions or implied through actions. When asked directly about rules, these children often added restrictions that were never imposed by the teacher. The observer (O) asked a five-year-old boy and girl (J and P) if there were any rules that must be followed in the playhouse.

> J: Fact 1: No running. Fact 2: Don't run outside. Fact 3: Don't dirty around this. Fact 4: Don't bring blocks in.
> O: Can you play anything you want in here?
> P: Yeah.
> J: No, you got to have the teacher's permission.
> O: But if the teacher says you can play out here?

J: Then we can pretend we're anything we want.

O: What if you each want to play different things?

J: Then she play one thing and I play another thing.

In some respects, these egocentric children resisted change, and the rules were considered fixed. Thus, they would complain when another child tried to adjust their structure, or take a block. In a few instances, unable to agree, they would call upon the teacher as the outside authority. In other ways it was interesting to observe how they appeared to be moving toward resolving their separate points of view. They were cooperating primarily through action, or out of the confusion of a dialogue, or through the power of one over the other.

Social Cooperation
(Concrete Operational Stage)

The children's rules or procedures for their play develop out of commonly practiced group goals, established by group consensus. There may, however, be discrepancies among individuals' understanding of rules. The rules are enriched through mutual exchange of ideas and actions. If one is loyal to the group, the rules must be respected. Procedures and roles may be changed, but only by swaying group opinion.

At the same time that children are gaining respect for a group perspective, they are developing internal controls which begin to replace adult constraints. The voluntary constraints brought about by the demands of play itself support this growth towards self control. Children at play, Vygotsky suggests, learn to subordinate themselves to rules by renouncing immediate wants as the route to maximum pleasure. Children may refuse, for example, to take a piece of candy, if they are modeling the role of a mother. It follows, Piaget proposes, that such a rule is an internal scheme, fostered by social interaction. It is the moral rule of self-restraint, not a rule obeyed like a physical law.

The following example of cooperative play originates from two seven-year-old girls.[19] They each flattened a piece of modeling clay which they decided to use as two islands. Then they began to make a connecting bridge.

S: I'll put this down here and you make the bridge.

(They both spend a little time shaping people.)

D: Well, I think that's pretty good. I'll put that here.

S: Yeah, that looks good. . . . How's this one?

D: OK. Make the body so it can stand.

(They are both rolling little balls and sticking appendages on them. S is making an intricate little face.)

D: Hey, if we're making a house, pretend that the roof is made out of straw, like Hawaii. (D makes a cube and sticks a pointed roof on it.)

S: We could pretend that it is Hawaii. (Her house.)

D: Make it so you can come out the door.

S: Here, you turn it around and make a door in it like this.

Rather than build separate islands, the two girls agreed to join them, maintaining a cooperative function.

In another observation, several boys were building a clubhouse and couldn't agree on a location for a sign which read "No Girls Allowed!" Since they never did agree, the sign was crumpled up. There remained, however, ample room for individual expression within the cooperative framework. A boy agreed to a suggested change in his building, but altered it according to his own taste.

The atmosphere for the development of rules with voluntary constraint is a crucial variable. Much of the play described here began without stated rules or regulations. The guidelines were only casually introduced as the need arose by any group member, not by one designated as a "rule giver!"

One paradox of play, Vygotsky suggests, is that here children adopt the line of least resistance; i.e., doing what is most fun. Children also learn to follow the line of greatest resistance; for by subordinating themselves to rules, children renounce immediate wants as the path to maximum pleasure in play. DeVries and Kamii have recently shown how group games, with external rule systems, also allow children to develop internal controls, independent of adult constraint.[20]

Implications for Social Studies

The growth toward social cooperation is primarily concerned with understanding another person's point of view. The child's ability to place herself or himself in "another person's shoes" only gradually appears through social interaction with peers and adults in a variety of settings. This ability is dependent partially upon the quality of experiences a child has had and upon the quality of the interaction. If children are honestly engaged in an activity of their own interest, the internal structure of rules develops as informally and as gradually as does their understanding of logical problems.

Knowledge about the stages of moral development and children's evolving understanding of rules are helpful to teachers as they assist children to make decisions about appropriate rules for classroom behavior, about guidelines for playing on the playground, and about other types of social interactions. Problems of conflict resolution through development of cooperative social patterns can be guided by the knowledgeable teacher. These and other aspects of moral judgments are further examined in Chapter Three.

Observation and Documentation: Methods and Implications

The fourth theme of the developmental approach is that of observation and documentation. These are important skills for both teachers and for children, but for different reasons. The teachers observe children to learn more about their stages of development. Children gain new cognitive and physical skills through active observation of their environment.

The teacher/observer can use several observation techniques. Piaget's clinical method of observing children's development is an appropriate starting point for conducting an objective analysis of children's social interaction. The central aim of this method is to uncover the trend, the basic structure of children's actions and social interactions. The observer may begin by focusing on one child, or on one activity, and regularly recording the language and actions that occur for a brief period each day or for several days. By examining one child's actions and environment as a whole piece, rather than separately, the observer is able to establish an inventory of that child's ideas and explanations. Such an inventory can also include samples of children's work. This documentation, gathered over a long term and including observations of the child in many situations, may then be used to determine patterns in that child's growth. It is this long-range view of the child's growth that will make it possible for the teacher to place the individual's developmental achievements into proper perspective.

A careful observation accompanied by an ongoing analysis of children, in partially structured problem settings and in the unstructured settings of the classroom, will give the teacher a framework for relating the theory of the active development of intelligence to the practical learning needs of children.

In order to establish a well-rounded inventory of the child's belief system and to determine overall patterns in development, the teacher will consider several aspects of development. In addition to recognizing the stages of development through the previously mentioned methods, children can also be observed at play. Observation of children at play helps identify the essential relationships between everyday social experiences and the development of intelligence, between social studies and the children themselves. Observations and discussions with children about the rules for their play will provide the basic data base for going beyond the stage-of-development interviews.

All of the above avenues for observing children have one prime goal—planning optimum educational environments for children. Piaget says that young children, early in their lives, should be provided with activities which would support the natural development of their powers of observation.[21] Brearley, in her work on integration of development and education, emphasizes that observation is an integral part of children's activities.[22] What children select in their observations is determined by the object or action being examined, and by their own points of view. Also, children's observations

are determined partly by past experience, which is personal and internalized, and partly by the test of reliability, a social act in which one's own observation is confirmed (or disputed) by other people's observations.

To encourage their observational learning, children may make charts and keep journals or prepare other types of records. Records may be kept on many processes and objects, including changes in plants or pets, growth in animals or children, or information related to selected community projects. These observations serve to develop an awareness of the children's own learning and to encourage growth towards the acceptance of another person's observation as a valid point of view.

The teacher's role in supporting children's observations of physical or social events is to provide ways to extend their thoughts and actions, to pose questions based on children's own questions, and to integrate experience and ideas through discussion and example. The gradual appearance of cooperation depends upon children's and adults' ability to understand another person's idea and to exchange meaning with one another.

Conclusion

iaget describes the dual role of action in the development of cooperation and intelligence in the following way:

When I say "active" I mean it in two senses. One is acting on material things, But the other means doing things in social collaboration, in a group effort. This leads to a critical frame of mind where children must communicate with each other. This is an essential factor in intellectual development. Cooperation is indeed co-operation.[23]

Adults who observe children regularly have become convinced of the importance of action and social interaction through organized activities and through informal play. These are the "building blocks" for the intellectual and social development of children. Social studies as the center of the early childhood education program provides many opportunities for learning and growing through action.

Footnotes

[1] Evelyn Weber, *The Kindergarten: Its Encounter with Educational Thoughts in America* (New York: Teachers College Press, 1969).

[2] John Dewey, *Democracy and Education* (New York: The Free Press, 1916/1966).

[3] Jerome Bruner, *Toward a Theory of Instruction* (Cambridge, Massachusetts: Harvard University Press, 1966); Hilda Taba and J. L. Hills, *Teacher Handbook for Contra Costra Social Studies* (Hayward, California: Rapid Printers and Lithographers, Inc., 1965).

[4] Bernard Spodek (ed.), *Open Education: The Legacy of the Progressive Movement* (Washington, D. C.: National Association for the Education of Young Children, 1970); Lillian Weber, *The English Infant School and Informal Education* (Englewood Cliffs, New Jersey: Prentice-Hall, 1965).

[5] O. W. Markley, "The New Image of Man," *The New York Times* (December 16, 1974).

[6] David Hawkins, "Messing About in Science," *Science and Children* 2:5 (February 1965).

[7] Lucy Sprague Mitchell, *Young Geographers* (New York: Bank Street College of Education, 1971). This book was first published in 1934.

[8] Carl W. Geraci, Principal, Lefferts Park Elementary School in Brooklyn, New York, is well known for building positive relations between his school and community, a community of several generations of Italian American families. He recounted this story of active involvement.

[9] Mitchell, *Young Geographers*, p. 30.

[10] Dewey, *Democracy and Education*.

[11] Lillian Weber, "Social Studies," *Insights into Open Education* 9 (October, 1976):3-8.

[12] Jean Piaget, *The Psychology of Intelligence* (London: Routledge & Kegan Paul, 1950).

[13] Jean Piaget, *The Moral Judgment of the Child* (London: Routledge & Kegan Paul, 1932); Lev Vygotsky, "Play and Its Role in the Mental Development of the Child," *Soviet Psychology* 5:3 (1967):6-18.

[14] Jean Piaget, *Child's Conception of the World* (Totowa, New York: Littlefield, Adams, and Company, 1960), p. 62.

[15] Bruner, *Toward a Theory*; Taba and Mills, *Teacher Handbook*; I. Sigel, *Child Development and Social Science Education: Parts I, II, III, and IV* (Lafayette, Indiana: Social Science Education Consortium, Purdue University, 1966).

[16] Jean Piaget and Barbel Inhelder, *The Psychology of the Child* (New York: Basic Books, 1969).

[17] Vygotsky, "Play and Its Role"; Piaget, *The Moral Judgment of the Child*.

[18] Piaget, *ibid.*

[19] Loren Weybright, *Piaget and Children's Play: The Teacher and Development*, Audio tape, 45 minutes (Fairlawn, New Jersey: The JAB Press, Inc., 1975); Loren Weybright, "The Teacher's Role in the Development of Play and Logical Thought," *The Urban Review* (Summer, 1976); Loren Weybright, "Young Children's Ideas About and Practice of Their Own Rules in Imaginative Play," *Piaget and the Helping Professions, Seventh Annual Conference Publication* (Los Angeles: University of Southern California, 1977). All children's conversations not otherwise credited are from these publications.

[20] Rita DeVries and Constance Kamii, *Why Group Games? A Piagetian Perspective* (Urbana, Illinois: ERIC Clearinghouse on Early Childhood Education, 1975).

[21] Jean Piaget, *To Understand Is To Invent* (New York: Grossman Publishers, Viking Compass Edition, 1973).

[22] Molly Brearley (ed.), *The Teaching of Young Children* (New York: Schocken, 1970).

[23] Piaget, *The Moral Judgment of the Child.*

2 Children Making Decisions and Solving Problems

Lois Wolf

Thinking, feeling, acting—these are three dimensions of behavior to which social education is addressed. Developing capacities to think on an abstract level and to make effective decisions; developing and enlarging the capacity for empathy; and developing abilities to act with judgment, caring, commitment—these are goals of social education which guide our curriculum decisions. Subordinate to the broader goals identified above are the objectives of effective decision-making and problem-solving which guide and shape daily practices and programs.

This chapter presents three curriculum episodes in preschool education. Each episode is analyzed for relationships to goals of developing problem-solving and decision-making skills in young children. Each episode is placed first in the context of the broadest goals of effective thinking, feeling, and acting, and then in the context of the particular goal of effective decision-making and problem-solving. Through the discussion of each episode, relationships between learning in the early years and that learning as the foundation for the rest of our lives become clear. The teacher of early childhood education can recognize situations that may serve as models for action in classroom planning.

Episode One:
Four-Year-Olds Build Their City

The following episode is an example of a project in which two teachers plan an "out of class" social studies activity and follow it up, over a period of time, with classroom activities intended to reinforce and expand social learning.

Jane Roger and Paolo Mendez, teachers of a class of four-year-olds, plan a walk to the construction site a block away from the school. They carry enough manila paper and crayons so that the children can sketch whatever interests them the most. They also take pads and pencils to jot down children's questions, conversations, and brief interviews of workers.

The next day when the children come into the room, they see big story charts up on the wall accompanied by their drawings and a few cut-out pictures to remind them of whom they had seen and what had happened.

Chart One:
The Fours Went to a Construction Site
We saw many workmen.
We saw their tools.
We saw their machines.
We had many questions.
Tommy: "What does that big truck do?"
Alison: "Why is water coming out of the ground?"
Greg: "How will they get those metal pieces down there?"
Robert: "What happens when you get tired?"
Betty: "How long have you been doing this job?"

Chart Two:
Paul, Giovanni, and David
Interviewed a Workman
His name was Mike.
Pauline: "What is the machine you're driving?"
Mike: "It's a back hoe."
Giovanni: "Was it hard to learn how to run the machine?"
Mike: "Well, not really. But I practiced for two weeks."
David: "How long will it take to build this building?
What will it be?"
Mike: "It will take eight months. It will be a new apartment house."

The Fours ask their teachers to read the chart over and over again. They love to hear the questions and they enjoy the repetition. They begin to say the chart out loud. They learn to recognize punctuation points, periods, and questions marks. They learn to recognize their names. The chart stimulates their thinking. They think of other questions they can ask when they revisit the construction site.

A few days later the teachers begin to relate the past experiences to a new situation in the classroom. "We can do some exciting block building," Jane suggests. (She leaves the statement open-ended and does not make specific decisions for the children ahead of time.) Paolo continues, "Be thinking of what you'll build." (In doing this he places the responsibility for action on the children, rather than on the teachers.)

Tommy and Greg quickly team up. "We're going to build the manager's house. We're going to have the manager standing near his house."

"How about you, Alison?" asks Paolo, bringing a reticent child into the conversation. Alison, Robert, and Molly talk together for a minute and then announce: "We're going to build the building!" Some children lose interest. They have other activities in mind.

But the block building is always popular and central to the learning of these four-year-olds. The space for building is one quarter of the room, enclosed on three sides by shelf after shelf of large wooden blocks of different shapes (mostly rectangular) and sizes. Accompanying shelves of block accessories flank the blocks—accessories such as transportation objects (trucks, cars, trains, boats); simple wooden furniture for the insides of houses; rubber people and community workers of varying ages, sex, and races; ropes, pulleys for elevators, and ramps for entrances and exits.

Block building takes place each day. All of the children are encouraged—indeed, expected—to participate each week. Sometimes written signs are needed, and then the teachers join in. Block building gives children the chance to work out problems of space, design, and construction. Block building lays foundations for social studies, mathematics, science, and language, in ways appropriate to four-year-olds' energies and interests.[1]

The six children who choose to work with blocks do so intensely and with gusto. Forty-five minutes pass. They bring in toy trucks, add people who are watching on the sidewalk, a few trees, and a bit of sand. Then they stand back and view their work with great satisfaction.

What does all of this activity mean? How does it relate to social education? John Dewey writes of the principle of *continuity of experience*—of the flowering and unfolding of experiences, one from another, extending the network of relationships—in an orderly manner throughout life.[2] When the four-year-olds observe a construction site, ask questions, talk together, see their teachers recording their words, hear their teachers read their words back, and re-create experiences in block building and dramatic play which get more and more elaborate as they proceed, they are learning in the most powerful way ever.

Episode Two:
Kindergarteners Listen to a Story

Twenty-five children, ages 5-1/2 to 6, sit quietly in a succession of half-circles on a soft rug. Their teacher, Ms. Banks, is settling into a rocker in front of them with *Crow Boy*, the book to be read today.[3] These kindergarteners love this time of day, at the end of their busy, active morning, just before lunch.

They relax, settle into a warmly related sharing time, and feel close to their teacher and to each other. They listen quietly and carefully as their teacher reads. The problem of the story is stated immediately:

> On the first day of our village school in Japan, there was a boy missing. He was found hidden away in the dark space underneath the schoolhouse floor. None of us knew him. He was nicknamed Chibi because he was very small. Chibi means "Tiny Boy."[4]

The children are taken in on the problem of a child who sees himself as different and behaves in such a manner that he becomes a complete isolate. Over the years in school he is rejected and ridiculed by those "others" who take him literally. "He was always at the

end of the line, always at the foot of the class, a forlorn little tag-along. . . ."[5]

The story continues. Crow Boy's problem increases over his years of schooling, from first to sixth grade. Although this story is set in Japan, a faraway setting, the problem itself is familiar, as is the context (of school) and the general set of expectations. Chibi's pain persists. His means of coping become highly developed.

> He would watch first the ceiling, then the wooden top of his desk, or a patch of cloth on a boy's shoulder. . .and Chibi found many ways, one after another, to kill time and amuse himself.[6]

Finally, in the sixth grade, Chibi's problem is revealed to his new teacher, Mr. Isobe. Mr. Isobe takes the children out to the hillside. He observes Chibi's involvement in and knowledge of natural life. He enjoys Chibi's calligraphy and his knowledge of "all the places where the wild grapes and wild potatoes grew."[7] He offers Chibi the opportu-

nity to display an unusual talent—imitating the voice of crows.

> Mr. Isobe explained how Chibi had learned those calls—leaving his home for school at dawn, and arriving home at sunset, every day for six long years. Everyone of us cried, thinking how much we had been wrong to Chibi all those long years.[8]

The five-year-olds have been completely absorbed. Their involvement in the story, their sharing of this experience, has great power. "Poor Chibi!" "They were so mean to him." "He should have fought back." "He was nice."

"Do you know anyone like Chibi?" asks Ms. Banks. She probes a bit to see if the children can relate Chibi to themselves and to those children they know. It is hard for young children to make this connection. They become bounded by each situation and do not move from the concrete to the abstract. Each situation stands by itself.

Ms. Banks stays with Chibi and encourages the children to ask questions, reflect, and elaborate on this story and this situation. She uses this opportunity, as during all their story times, to encourage children's language experiences, use of vocabulary, sense of chronology, and exploration of character, setting, mood, plot. She gets them to ask questions about Japan: where it is, who lives there, what the people look like, how they dress, etc. Her own knowledge of Japan is an asset to her as she responds to the children's questions. But the predominant concern of the children is for Chibi, the sad, forlorn, little tag-along. Their sympathies and capacities for empathy have been activated and nourished during this storytelling time.

> The dimension of empathy, like all developmental strands, is a long time "in the making." The development of "humanness," of which empathy is a key ingredient, cannot begin at age eight or twelve or twenty. Unless foundations are laid in infancy and in the early years, developmental gaps prevent full flowering—and often completely obliterate human capacities.[9]

The classroom teacher used this everyday occurrence of storytelling to build foundations for empathy and concern in the children.

Episode Three: Preschoolers Share the Clean-Up Campaign

"EveryChild" Day Care Center, housing children from three to five, is located on the second floor of a settlement house in an inner-city neighborhood. It is early fall, and the air is crisp and clear. Leaves are turning a spectrum of colors. One jarring intrusion into an otherwise beautiful scene on the block is litter. Candy wrappers, leftover orange peels, beer cans in the gutter, deposits of dog feces, newspaper scraps, an old shoe, and other rubbish greet the children as they enter the school each day.

Although the children are very young, the director of the center, together with teachers and parents, shares a commitment to social action projects as part of the curriculum. Staff and parents meet regularly—once a month—and more often for special needs, to explore and plan for identified problems. The

October agenda is headed by the problem of sanitation; i.e., the litter on the block. Questions are brought up at the meeting and discussed.

1. What is the nature of the litter?
2. Where does all this litter come from? Businesses? Residents? Passersby?
3. Who is doing it? Certain people? A few? Many?
4. When do people litter? All the time? Weekdays? Weekends? Mornings? Evenings?
5. What areas get littered? Selective spots? Everywhere?
6. How can the problem be solved?

The parents and staff become more involved as the discussion progresses. They break up into small groups, with each group talking about one or two of the questions. One task is to outline possible ways for the children to participate in community action to deal with this problem.

Although staff and parents have gone through an important process of identifying and analyzing the problem followed by a plan for solution, it is now necessary to go through some of these same steps of problem-solving with the children. Ms. Anne Scott, the Director, presents the problem to the children in a brief assembly. She asks for suggestions, and children respond eagerly. Carlos tells about all the beer cans in the street. "Men drink beer and throw the cans away," he explains. Paulina agrees.

"What else do we see on the sidewalks and in the street?" asks Ms. Scott, seeking to extend their thinking through questions. Four-year-old Herman asserts loudly, "Dog doo! Ugh! My mother always says to watch where you step."

The children are getting excited and restless, eager to tell something of their own, to enter into this discussion. Ms. Scott, however, suggests that this was an excellent beginning and recommends that the children discuss these problems in their classes and try to find some solutions. All of them can report their progress at another group meeting next Wednesday.

On Wednesday morning, children and adults come together to report on their progress. Preplanning by the teachers helped designate particular problems for each group.

This gave the children freedom to act, but within a specified limit. The Threes focused on: What litter is found on the street? They gave considerable evidence, which the teachers wrote down on a big chart entitled "Litter—What It Is." Their chart included items that they had remembered seeing; but in the coming week, it would be their responsibility to keep a record, a survey, of what litter was currently on the street. The teacher would help them make a big list of what they see.

The Fours concentrated on particular sites of litter. They decided that they will station children with a teacher outside the entrance of the school. They will have ten-minute shifts throughout the morning. They will watch *where* people and animals deposit litter and report to the teacher, who will keep a map of the street. Then they will paint a larger version of the map to bring to the next assembly. The Fours will also note *who* is leaving litter. They will check this information off on simple charts, which their teachers will have made up for them.

The five-year-olds are to suggest ways of solving the problem. They get together in large groups and small groups. As they pool their ideas, the teacher keeps notes. They go out for a walk to look at ways in which the city attacks the problem. They see trash cans, sewer-drains, hydrants, sprinkler trucks, big plastic garbage bags, and garbage trucks. They visit the waste disposal plant. Some children tell how their relatives in rural areas dispose of garbage. They compose a group letter to the Sanitation Commissioner and also to the neighborhood storekeepers. They plan to visit storekeepers in the future.

In the meantime, the parents and staff plan for a block party to include residents and businesses. They hope and expect that a community network will emerge from this project which will act as a small but important force for positive community action.

At the next assembly, all the groups are ready with reports, graphs, charts, murals, maps, and letters. After the reports are given and some discussion is held, it is decided that the children will build two wooden trash cans in which large plastic bags will be placed. They will paint the cans and put the school's name on them. They will also take turns hosing down the gutter and bagging the litter each day. The wooden trash cans will be displayed at the block party.

This episode of community action involved teachers, parents, staff, and children. Children participated in the collection of information, decision-making, and problem-solving with adults in a neighborhood project.

Analysis of Goals of Social Education

Effective thinking, deep feeling, informed action—if these are overriding goals for social education, then how do our three episodes move toward these goals?

We have learned over many years that intellectual, emotional, and social developments proceed in stages, one leading into the next, held constant over time, although varying according to each individual. The young child of ages three through six must gather storehouses of data about the world—identifying objects, places, people, events—before moving on to put these items together into meaningful contexts.[10]

Thus, in the preschool years a great effort goes into identification of color, shape, days of weeks, months, seasons, numerals, names of foods, and animals. Four-year-olds go on trips regularly to identify people, objects, and work processes in their own familiar environments. Construction, bulldozers, cranes, pulleys, steel beams, foundations, workers, foremen, architects, and plans become familiar words to them. They compare the real people and objects with pictures in books and in matching games. Then, when they re-create their experience in blocks, they talk with their teachers about what they have built, why they need ramps, why they need pulleys, what the pulleys will lift, and what the ramps will facilitate. They put trucks and people near the construction site and do their best to match the toy trucks with the pictures in their books.

The richer the foundation of information in these years, the more effective children's thinking will be as they move from what Piaget calls pre-operational to concrete operational thinking in the middle years of childhood (usually ages eight to eleven).

Just as with the development of thought,

emotions must also extend and deepen as children get older. The young child is ego-centric—seeing the world in his or her image, bounded by very limited personal experience. At first, the infant is not separate from the nurturing parents. Slowly, separation occurs, and the parent gains constantly as the child reaches the first year. In these earliest years, the issue of trust emerges, trust based upon predictability and nurturance.[11]

The constancy of the nurturing parent develops into the nurturance and love for the tiny explorer and adventurer, the toddler. By the time our toddler grows to be three, then four and five, parent surrogates, even peers, perform the functions of constant interaction and nurturing relationships. When Ms. Banks, the kindergarten teacher, reads *Crow Boy*, she is providing an important dimension of nurturance—a shared social experience within which young children can learn about people through the process of identification. In this way, they experience feeling for another which is validated by their classmates' feelings. All the children feel for—and with—Chibi. All the children delight in Chibi's accomplishment and eventual triumph.

Certainly through the middle grades, reading stories to children builds a rich foundation of shared feeling and a springboard for discussion. Children learn, on the one hand, how like everyone else they are; and they learn this by sharing experiences, verbally expressing their feelings and responses to their shared experiences, communicating this expression to peers and to nurturing adults, and listening and responding to the expressions of others.

In positive classroom environments, they can also learn that each person—each one of them—is unique, just a little bit different from everyone else. But these differences contribute to a richness and vitality in the group, not to a loss of strength.

The balance between our common traits of humanness and our unique traits is revealed in the earliest years of our lives, and can be—must be—reinforced and sharply delineated in early schooling. In later years, children who benefit from early experiences of this nature are able to try out options; i.e.,

take multiple roles in their work and personal lives.

Informed action rests on the nature of democratic process and years of experience in collaborative problem-solving and decision-making. Wolf writes of the group democratic process: "Two spheres of influence exist; interaction between peers and interaction between peers and leaders. In democratic groups, the nature of peer group interaction is collaborative, reciprocal and mutual. The group adds to the individual, the individual adds to the group."[12]

In *Democracy and Education*, Dewey writes:

> A democracy is more than a form of government; it is primarily a mode of associated living, of conjoint communicated experience. The extension in space of a number of individuals who participate in an interest so that each has to refer his own action to that of others, and to consider the action of others to give point and direction to his own, is equivalent to the breaking down of these barriers of class, race and national territory which kept men from perceiving the full import of their activity.[13]

He sums up the characteristics of democracy as:

> The widening of the area of shared concerns, the liberation of a greater diversity of personal capacities.[14]

The episode of the cleanup campaign illustrates how children and adults can share a widening area of concerns, thus liberating a range of personal "capacities."

Teaching/Learning Strategies

That teaching/learning strategies can teachers employ to build toward skills and attitudes necessary for problem-solving and decision-making? Holding *regular discussion times*, no matter how short in duration, from the earliest years on, is central. Even in the early years, when children are in democratic environments, they learn to ask questions (preferably open-ended questions); they learn to converse, to elaborate on points made, and to deepen and extend contexts. *Recording* statements, questions, discussions, interviews, and reflections plays back to children their own thoughts, ideas, and feelings. They can laugh together, elaborate, correct, chant the words together, and, most important, remember back to their shared original experience and the subsequent discussion of it.

Block-building, as a central method in early childhood social education, came into being when Caroline Pratt, a progressive education pioneer, developed the City and Country School in New York's Greenwich Village in the 1920s.[15] Now unit blocks are found in preschool classrooms throughout the world. Their power, as material and the activity which ensues therefrom, rests on the open-ended, unstructured nature of blocks, the need to use imagination and problem-solving methods to utilize them effectively, their endless possibilities in recreating experience of the real world, and the range and depth of learning which takes place on many levels. *Reading books* and *telling stories* to young children are other strategies for learning. The oral/aural mode demands activity from the children. Unlike the passive, narcotic-like state that television may induce, particularly from excessive use, listening to stories keeps children's minds active, busy imagining scenes and situations. "What picture do you see in your mind when I read about Chibi walking home over miles and miles of country roads?" asks Ms. Banks. "What colors do you see, what sounds do you hear, what noises do the crows make?"

Gathering information about the litter requires going outside and *observing,* then *recording,* either on *charts,* or on *graphs,* or on *maps,* or on *murals. Interviewing* is central to this task of problem-solving. A good interviewer requires *sensitive questions* and a *logical sequence.* Participant observation is an important mode of study used by social scientists from Margaret Mead to Robert Coles to William L. Whyte. Children learn the beginnings of such methods by acquiring attitudes of respect for those whom they interview and by reflection about what they ask.

Writing letters, *building* trash cans, and *cleaning* streets are all strategies necessary to this problem-centered study of the environment and its pollution. Coming together in *assemblies,* town-meeting style, reinforces the importance of this study for all of the children and supports their work with their parents' involvement.

The most important strategy in the social studies learning of young children is the use of *real problems* for the content. The current and pervasive concern for an environment free of industrial pollution transcends age, class, and national boundaries. Garbage and waste disposal, particularly in urban areas. presents a growing problem. Litter on the street is one manifestation of this problem. By using such a reality-based situation, our youngest children begin to develop a base of knowledge, a repertoire of skills, and constructive attitudes toward living in today's complex technological society.

As teachers consistently build curricula which use real-life problem-centered episodes, employ methods resting on democratic group process and provide a wide range of materials yielding rich insights into one's self and others, we may help our children move toward the central social studies goals of effective thinking, depth of feeling, and committed action.

Footnotes

[1] Elizabeth S. Hirsch, editor, *The Block Book* (Washington, D. C.: National Association for the Education of Young Children, 1974).

[2] John Dewey, *Experience and Education* (New York: Macmillan & Co., 1938).

[3] Taro Yashima, *Crow Boy* (New York: The Viking Press, 1955), pp. 4, 5.

[4] *Ibid.*

[5] *Ibid.*

[6] *Ibid.*

[7] *Ibid.*

[8] *Ibid.*

[9] Lois C. Wolf, "Children's Literature and the Development of Empathy in Young Children," *Journal of Moral Education* 5 (October 1975):45-49.

[10] Lois C. Wolf, "The Development of Levels of Abstraction in Children's Thinking About Complex Social Problems." A paper presented to the American Educational Research Association, 1975.

[11] Erik H. Erikson, *Childhood and Society* (New York: Norton, 1953).

[12] Lois C. Wolf, "Democratic Group Process and Early Schooling. A paper presented to the National Council in Social Studies, 1975.

[13] John Dewey, *Democracy and Education* (New York: The Free Press, 1944), pp. 86, 87.

[14] *Ibid.*

[15] Caroline Pratt, *I Learn from Children* (New York: Simon and Schuster, 1948).

3
Children
Becoming Citizens

Nancy Wyner

If you ask a six-year-old what rules are, the child might reply, "They tell you what to do or not to do!" A six-year-old might also talk about how frightening it is when one doesn't know what the rules are, or even how to keep them when they are hard to understand and remember. Or try asking about the flag, symbol of our national identity. The following fragments are from informal conversations with children in early childhood programs.

Four-year-old Barney sang his version of "The Star Spangled Banner" to his uncle.

"What's that?" his uncle asked.

"It's the Phillies' theme song!" the boy replied.

These are responses to the question "What is a flag?" given by five- and six-year-olds.

Alice:	Something Betsy Ross made.
Bob:	She discovered it.
Alice:	No, she didn't, she sewed it.
Charles:	Yah, 'cause China has a flag.
Alice:	France has a flag too.
Charles:	I know there's a President flag.
Dorothy:	A flag is a flag!
Ed:	It's a piece of cloth that is sort of a symbol of the country.
Dorothy:	Yah, it's like cloth with things sewed onto it, stars, stripes, or anythin' you want.

Six-year-olds respond to the question "Why do we have flags?"

Alice:	Well, I guess it represents the country.
Bob:	It represents the nation.
Charles:	So they can tell countries apart from each other.
Alice:	They have 'em so you can tell what country they are.
Dorothy:	If you wanna know so bad, go look in a flag book!

In watching and listening to such rich accounts gathered from informal discussions with young children, we can begin to understand the remarkable range of the child's information, and especially the child's particular view of the legal/political world in which we live. These protocols offer some insight into the "intuitive political thinking" of the child, whose views are far more interesting, more knowing, and more revealing of the child's developmental stages than we might have imagined. Children's statements help us to gain insight into their active, creative involvement in the development of their own beliefs. They turn our focus to the child's search for meaning through interactions in family, school, and other settings.

In this chapter we will consider some of the sources and influences that shape the child's view of the political world, examining the context of early education as foundations for adult citizen actions. Particular emphasis will center on the school as an environment for developing understandings and behaviors essential for our unique social/political system, American democracy. Emerging viewpoints about the young child as an active learner in the political environment will be discussed. Early competencies for citizenship, teaching modules, and resources will be proposed.

Introduction

Until recently, childhood has been regarded as a political void, and little evidence has accumulated of the meanings and thoughts of this nascent political person, the young child. Yet the experiences children encounter are enormously complex, and their efforts to unravel and give meaning to them are considerable. Professor Judith Torney's work helps us to understand the child's developing view of the political environment: "Elementary school children require a great deal of help in understanding what a pluralistic system is, in learning to value its diversity, and in comprehending how a system operates and persists over time, often with the help of criticism and the resolution of conflicting ideas."[1]

There is a critical need to understand how young children acquire social and political attitudes and skills that become the basis of their relatedness to the political system, understandings that will lead to careful, thoughtful educational responses to preparing future generations for active citizenship. The process of merely teaching children facts, historical dates, and unquestioned doctrine "tells them little about the values and processes of democracy. To impart only slogans to children—particularly nationalistic ones—provides inadequate preparation for active, participant citizenship which occurs in interactions with other people and is guided by mutual expectations."[2]

Connell, an Australian developmental psychologist, has produced a collective portrait of a group of Australian children that deals with the development of the child's relationships with the social world and aspects of his or her political reasoning about it. In this study, "The Child's Construction of Politics," Connell takes an approach that differs from conventional ways of thinking about how we socialize children into the political system. He attempts to establish some of the social bases of political commitment, and makes evident in his research that at some point the child does begin to form a sense of self in the political environment.[3] Not unlike ethnic self-concept and race awareness that find roots in early preschool experience, it is increasingly clear that early childhood is a formative period for the rapid development of the concept of the political self, a sense of self marked by growing attitudes about how the system works. The ingathering of experiences and the shaping of attitudes through interactions in the environment are part of the process of children becoming citizens, setting foundations for adult citizen actions. Robert Coles presses the point when he asks:

> Why do we so often assume that it takes ten or twenty years for children to begin to understand exactly what it is that works for or against them in the world; meaning, more concretely, which politicians stand for what, and more broadly, how the assumptions of a given social and political order will quite specifically affect their future lives?[4]

In actuality, these assumptions are imprecise and outdated if we are to take emerging research seriously. For although we might characterize the young child's thinking as subjective, fanciful, intuitive, or muddled, Piaget reminds us that the process is active and continuous. Knowledge of children's perceptions and misconceptions can be an important source for directing efforts to organize learning experiences for them. Knowledge of children's political thinking can also alert us to examine what we do teach, and what we ought to be teaching to help the child in becoming a citizen.

The Setting for Becoming a Citizen: Schooling and Other Influences on the Child's View of the Political World

Citizenship education has been a recurring theme and a new trend since the nineteenth century, when early school reformers pressed forceful arguments for binding new immigrants to the republic by emphasizing and intensifying the influence of the school as an alternative to parental influence. What social harmony educators sought to achieve was embedded in the regulatory schooling experiences that were to become familiar to generations of Americans. Children of immigrant families in search of a new national identity were taught immutable truths, unquestioned facts complemented by patriotic anthems and rituals. Through practice of punctuality and conformity to rules, they learned acquiescence to authority. Democracy was their ideal, and the hope of entering America's growing industrial workforce was the reality that shaped behaviors and the purpose of schooling. Almost a century later, Coles, who has been working for two decades with children of various backgrounds in every region of this country, reflected on the same poignant theme of national identity:

> I have sometimes wondered what, if anything, binds them together even a little—gives them a sense of being, after all, Americans, whatever their differences. Is there anything remotely substantial that an Eskimo child, say, or a black child of migrant farm worker parents, has in common with a boy or girl whose father is a corporation lawyer or a business executive with a home in a quiet and comfortable town, well outside of Boston—or New York, or Chicago, or Atlanta? [5]

What does citizenship mean to young children? And how can schooling help, even in the very early years of childhood, to give our children a sense of being Americans, involving them in the continuing evolution and invention of a democratic society, guiding them toward understanding the discipline of freedom and toward valuing diversity, conveying to them a sense of the possibilities of our national society in the broader context of global society, and teaching them the skills and knowledge necessary for participation in tomorrow's world?

Children are learning about citizenship—about fairness, participation, and responsibility—in the seeming randomness of the playground, the bus ride to school, encounters with the crossing guard, supper time discussions with the family, group discussions in the classroom, games at physical education/recreation time, and watching television. Lawrence Cremin captures the thought when he observes:

> The important fact is that family life does educate, religious life does educate, and work does educate; and, what is more, the education of all three realms is as intentional as the education of the school, though in different ways and in different measures. [6]

In actuality, the schools are only one example of society's power to educate, and any full accounting of the child's learning experiences, any curricular response to teaching the child about citizenship must consider the various environments in which the child travels about. Planning a contemporary curricular response that acknowledges the expanding range of interactions and information sources available to the young child is a rigorous task. Planning must also respond to themes that will dominate future realities of these youngsters. The classroom teacher's response to the total needs of the child include a recognition of several areas important to citizenship in the world of the future.

For example, *conflict* is a persistent reality of life. Our educational institutions can make constructive use of conflict episodes to teach democratic approaches to the struggles between individual and societal needs. Awareness of conflict floods through to the child from seemingly random events. Most assuredly, children have grasped a schema of conflict from the general environment in which they live, the group games they play, the comic books they read, and the television programs they watch.

As teaching adults, we search for ways of converting conflict episodes into growth-promoting understandings. We look for ways of helping children become more aware and more rationally attuned to these events in order to offset, avoid, or resolve similar problems at a later time. The battles on the playground over telling, lying, losing, bullying, and racism; and the daily trouble spots in the classroom over cheating, stealing, unfairness, pushing, shoving, bossing, and outright physical abuse are commonplace conflict events in children's lives. Children need to know the reasoned, concerned adult responses to these and other events of conflict and violence: how conflict is abhorred; the efforts taken to defuse and resolve conflict; and the attempts to settle conflict by using reasoned authority, discussion, negotiation, compromise, rulemaking, and policy formation as democratic processes.

The basic due-process approach provides an excellent format for teaching these skills, since emphasis is placed on the context in which the child is taught the skills as well as the processes. This process includes the following actions to assist the teacher in conflict management:

1. *Two-party meetings.* The teacher will take aside a dissatisfied or disruptive child for a low-keyed talk. The focus is

on clarifying what has happened. For example, Donna says, "Jane took all the Magic Markers and she won't let me use them, so I just took them when she wasn't looking!" Perhaps a discussion between teacher and child will be sufficient to find a workable solution for future action. Together they can determine what steps need to be taken to resolve the immediate problem as well.

Other opportunities for two-party meetings involve the teacher as initiator in bringing together two children to talk things over by themselves. This method is more effective for older primary children than it is for young children who are still very egocentric.

2. *Three-party meetings.* This involves the teacher as mediator or arbitrator listening carefully to each side, helping children express their own feelings and opinions about what has happened and encouraging them to listen to each other. Listening is especially important in these interactions since it will become the basis of any action.

3. *Group meetings.* Group meetings involve the teacher and the children who are directly involved in the problem. The teacher helps all children express themselves and leads the group in the decision-making process of finding an acceptable resolution.

Guidelines for managing conflict resolution include the following aspects:

1. What are the *facts* in the conflict episode? Facts are important, not only as a basis for action but for teaching the children the difference between what they think happened, what actually happened, and what needs to happen for smooth interactions in group life.

2. How do children *feel* about the situation? In many situations it is impossible to ascertain the facts. But emotional perceptions of the events are important to the resolution of the conflict. For example, in the problem between Donna and Jane, feelings may have been important to the resolution. Donna may have felt that Jane was unfair or that everyone in the class takes the markers and she never has a turn.

Bringing these feelings into the open clarifies the underlying motives for the disruption. When Donna realizes that the teacher knows she felt rejected, the first step to a resolution of the problem has occurred.

3. What fair *solutions* are possible? Children are very capable of suggesting creative and reasonable ways to resolve conflicts. Does Donna believe that she solved the problem by taking the markers away from Jane? Was there a better way to have a turn? In an interactive situation, the teacher expresses a belief that the children can come up with appropriate solutions. Children are encouraged to make suggestions. These can be written on a chalkboard or just accepted verbally. Then they can be reviewed for a final decision on the best response. Whatever course of action is taken, the teacher's consistent, supportive guidance will assure a balanced and fair social process.

4. Does the solution need a *revision?* An appeals process, or a reassessment of the past decision, is a way the teacher and the children can reconsider, discuss, and change past decisions that do not seem to be working. This step provides flexibility for dynamic social interactions. Conflict resolution is an ongoing process that gives children a way to solve human relations problems with a minimum of hostility and a maximum of satisfaction for all who are involved. It is a form of democratic action.

Scarcity of resources is a crucial issue in the global community. Within the spacious generalities of liberty and freedom, future citizens will need to make important decisions regarding the equitable, cooperative, and sensible use of resources in our environment. Our schools, as public institutions, can be important agencies for helping children become planners involved with the creation of policy and practice for their own lifespace, giving careful thought to how much and what to consume and to the social consequences of resource usage. From the global network of news media, young children are learning about starvation, drought in the Sahara and California, shortages of oil and the energy crisis, the Maine Indians' land claim, and the 200-mile fishing limit. These are all government policy issues and citizen-oriented subject matter. In today's world, they are also issues of interest to young children.

Often enough we emphasize the damaging consequences of *change and mobility,* and we underestimate the strength that can emerge from striving to master, to integrate, and to find meaning and useful purpose through a broadened range of experiences. Teachers can often bridge the gap between the familiar and the new by helping children recognize what may be familiar, although in a different context. Teachers can assist children in planning for changes so that they feel an underlying continuity in the change. For example, when children move away, a "round-robin" letter (even if the letter consists of pictures) helps the child to make a transition to the new community and assists the remaining children to adjust to the loss of their friend. Changes provide opportunities for new growth and new learning. As children look for changes in their own neighborhoods, they can learn about the reality of change in the broader world. As they observe changes in themselves (new learnings, new skills, new growths), they can become aware of ongoing changes in society. Changes in their lifetimes will probably occur more rapidly and with more intensity than in the life spans of their teachers, but we can prepare them for the complexities, the ambiguities, and the management of these changes.

Another dominant emerging theme to which we often given thoughtful attention is *interdependence in a global context,* a context in which a national identity is developed. In some clearminded way, we want to come to terms with the fragile conditions of world peace and the importance of orienting children to social responsibility and interdependence based on the mutuality of human need and human purpose. This finds a beginning in the classroom through a recognition of the many ways children depend upon others. They depend upon Ms. Brown to prepare their lunch; they depend upon Ms. Collins to drive their school bus; and they depend upon Mr. Bacon to open the school before they arrive in the morning. Johnnie needs to use Robert's pencil, and Betsy holds the door for Margaret. The teacher depends upon the children to assist her at snack time, to help pick up the toys, and to place their name cards on the attendance chart. Learning about interdependence starts with the daily relationships in which the children are involved. Respect for and appreciation of children with different ethnicity and cultures are included in preparing children to build world peace in the future.

In a large measure, American democracy is more than a form of government, a set of laws and constructs. It is more basically a mode of life, of conjoined experiences that serve as the basis for action in a diverse world community. Finding the common ground, constructing the common roof that will house our multiple values, nurturing mutual respect and obligation, and encouraging creative solutions to social problems and rational thought as a basis for participation are ideas that energize our efforts.

The Learning Child Becoming a Citizen

A perspective central to a contemporary conceptualization of citizenship as planned learning must consider the *child as learner.* Until recently, we have had to draw on ideas that dichotomized learning as either cognitive or affective. The developmental-interaction viewpoint, proposed by Barbara Biber with other colleagues, is an outgrowth of the ideas of Dewey and Piaget, and it offers a highly integrative approach to understanding growth processes.[7] It is an approach based on knowledge of the growing child and increased recognition of the role of the environment in learning. A basic tenet of this formulation is that "the growth of cognitive functions—acquiring and ordering information, judging, reasoning, problem solving, using systems of symbols—cannot be separated from the growth of personal and interpersonal processes—the development of self-esteem and a sense of identity, internalization of impulse control, capacity for autonomous response, [and] relatedness to other people. The interdependence of these developmental processes is the 'sine qua non' of the developmental-interaction approach."[8]

The following anecdote provides sharp testimony to the young child's struggle and to the need for a pluralistic, yet integrative, approach to citizenship education. The question directed to seven- and eight-year-olds is: "What is the Pledge of Allegiance?"

Ann: What is it?

Bob: You say it to the flag.

Carl: It's the National Anthem.

Bob: No, it isn't, stupid, some people say it before class starts.

Dan: We had to do it before class with a substitute. She made us put your hand over your heart, "I pledge allegiance to" . . . like that.

Bob: We said it before the gymnastics show.

Carl: No, that was the National Anthem. You sing that.

Ann: But it is a song.

Carl: No, it isn't.

Ann: Yes, it is!

Carl: No, it isn't!

Ann: All right, then, you should watch the hockey game on TV, the lady sings it all the time.

Bob: I don't know why we say it.

Dan: You say it when you are supposed to be saluting the flag.

Bob: It's queer because sometimes you say it, sometimes you don't. We always have to do it for the substitute; for the teacher you don't.

This scant, multilayered fragment of a group discussion conveys the remarkable range of sources for children's thinking, and an insight into the child's awareness of adults' inconsistency and conflicting, rather ambivalent, feelings toward teaching the symbols of national identity. It is evident that adult behaviors in the total environment do become a part of the individual child's repertoire and political consciousness. Triggered by their search for consistency and perceiving inconsistency, young children yield clues to our pluralistic value system. These youngsters seem to be quite clearly reading the environment and noting how strange it is in its inconsistency.

An anecdote such as this one, to quote Connell, "opens the tap of an interior monologue in which political figures, cartoon figures, familiar figures, fact and legend, jostle each other with splendid promiscuity."[9] This and other fragments gathered from American youngsters provide us with a sense of the child's way of knowing and perceiving an intricately organized political world. The construction goes on with continuity from childhood to adolescence. Connell characterizes the period to the age of seven as a "political prologue" in which the child's intuitive thinking lacks synthesizing power, a time in which early experiences inform an emerging political consciousness. The period marks the beginning of the child's efforts to build an interpretive structure, using as materials the bits and pieces of information culled from the media, random experience, and personal observation. At age seven or eight, according to Connell's study, the child comes to master factual information and to distinguish a political and governmental world from other areas of life. There is increasing effort at this time to conceptualize with increasing objectivity about political roles and responsibilities of special people in the political environment—for example, the police officer, the President, and other authorities, both local and national.

Curriculum and teaching experiences must consider these developmental processes and stimulate growth by providing children with accurate information and sufficient opportunities to learn social and political competencies through interaction within an expanding environment.

The Nature of Group Life in the Classroom

The social process itself is educating children, as is seen by the following discussion between a teacher and several children.

Teacher: What if people don't get along in a group?

Arnie: They should go into a different group.

Barb: If . . . uh . . . they fail in number one, then they should go to number two; and if they can't, they should go to number three.

Arnie: Yeh. Some people have to go to group 1000.

This fragment captures the children's sense of how hard it is to belong. They imag-

ine that you might fail forever, or at least have to go "to group 1000," without questioning whether people could *learn* to get along. Schooling that focuses on narrowly conceived cognitive tasks, preoccupied by testing, may emphasize academic achievement (or failure) as a major factor in belonging.

Most early childhood programs recognize the importance of social learning and the need to help children develop basic interpersonal competencies that enable them to feel and act as effective individuals and group members. Yet, we must be mindful of styles for belonging that each of us has. Lewis Thomas, the biologist, observes, "It is not a simple thing to decide where we fit, for at one time or another in our lives we manage to organize in every imaginable social arrangement. We are as interdependent, especially in our cities, as bees or ants, yet we can detach if we wish and go live alone in the woods, in theory anyway."[10]

In developing a child's sense of belonging, of how to get along in group life as preparatory experience for later social-citizen roles, teachers create supportive conditions in the classroom. Supportive environments provide:

1. for individual learning styles, intellectual and social interests and capabilities;
2. some degree of personal freedom involving the opportunity to express one's own ideas and point of view—to disagree, to think differently, and to feel differently;
3. continuing support as a valued group member;
4. opportunity to express some degree of privacy—in terms of space, personal belongings, and feelings;
5. ample opportunity to develop pro-social, interpersonal competencies through role taking, group discussions, and peer interactions; and
6. protection from sexism, racism, bigotry, and physical harm.

The Role of the Teaching Adult

Morality is that which supports life, immorality is simply that which tends to kill. Human beings are healthy in some situations. Like you take a little kid and every time he comes around you scream at him, he's going to grow up kind of crooked. You take a little kid, and every time he turns around you love him or, if necessary, you're stern with him though clearly loving; that makes a strong grown-up that's healthy.—John Gardner[11]

Certainly, as teachers, we are not the only adults who have the chance to be either clearly loving or "stern with him though clearly loving," yet teachers are critically important influences on the child's perceptions of authority. And "authority" is a basic concept of our political environment. Teachers, as authorities, model for children how power can be used by those who nurture cognition. In the early formative years, interactions between teacher and the child resonate with particular significance. According to Biber and Shapiro, "A major task is to establish the child's trust in himself, in the teacher, and in the school, since the mutual trust between the teacher and the child is the precondition for a supportive authority role."[12] Seeking effective application of authority in the helping/teaching relationship is a critical point in establishing self-discipline and healthful citizenship development.

To promote healthful citizenship education, the classroom teacher looks for ways to:

1. respond to the child as an individual;
2. encourage development of democratic behaviors through *planned* instruction that emphasizes teaching, learning, and using generic democratic processes (for example, open group discussion; decision-making through consensus, advocacy, voting, majority rule; and conflict management through negotiation and compromise);
3. establish clear boundaries, limits for behavior, emphasizing the reasoned need for rules and limits in the interests of the child and the group;
4. organize learning activities with deliberate attention to the child's repertoire of real-life experiences, encouraging children to observe, re-enact, reconstruct, and represent, in order to acquire knowledge, skills, and perspectives about our democratic political environment;
5. promote multicultural concepts through example and in all phases of the curriculum;
6. take an integrative approach that draws on child development concepts, the heritage of our political system, and the unique characteristics of the child's environment;
7. care about and act to develop mutual trust, self-discipline, and democratic participation.

Through these efforts, the quality of life in our society ought to be enhanced.

Curricular and Teaching Responses to Children Becoming Citizens

As we begin to reconceptualize education for citizenship with a curriculum for classroom teaching, we look for program planning that supports content and process-oriented learning and evaluation that "will foster an image of the classroom as a field consisting of multiple interactions and dynamics which have a great variety of consequences," and which include long- and short-term goals.[13] The following steps have been designed to clarify a program of citizenship education. They include:

1. delineation of *guiding principles* (Figure 1)
2. specification of appropriate citizenship *competencies* (Figure 2)
3. description of feasible *enabling processes* (Figure 3)
4. *evaluation* processes

The competencies are specified in two interrelated areas. Their construction is largely influenced by the writings of Piaget, Biber, Selman, and Torney,[14] and by the additional writings cited at the end of this chapter.

The competencies and enabling processes that have been specified emphasize what the child is to learn, as well as basic processes that enable the child to learn how to learn. Increasingly, research emphasizes that ultimately what is taught to young children, both the process for establishing the content and the content itself, shapes basic predispositions toward one's own group, toward diverse ethnic, racial and religious groups, and toward foreign people.[15]

Since the system of values implied by evaluative strategies controls the options and alternatives open to the curriculum planner and teacher, evaluative techniques can, and usually do, impact heavily on programs. It is therefore critical that evaluation instruments include recording classroom observations, documentation of the multiple events of the learning experience, and techniques yet to be developed that further support and extend the expressed intentions of the teacher and the transactions of the learner.

Summary

Effective educational programs in citizen education must recognize that the child is, inexorably, *becoming* a citizen. As responsible members of this society, we must make this growth process increasingly more rational. The commitment in this endeavor is not for the teacher alone, although teachers have a special interest and responsibility because of their influential roles. Teachers can facilitate citizen education through the process of daily living in the classroom and through careful planning of content that develops a knowledge-base for citizenship.

Responsive programs ought to involve the total community, helping diverse social institutions to define and develop complementary roles that support the child's learning experience and the efforts of educators. This is not a task for a year or two, but involves a continuous and long-range effort in which all participants change and grow.

Footnotes

[1] Judith V. Torney, "Child Development, Socialization and Education," National Science Foundation Elementary Political Education Project, Commissioned Paper Number 11 (Washington, D.C.: U.S. Government Printing Office, April 1973):4.

[2] Bernard Spodek, "Curriculum Construction in Early Childhood Education," in *Early Childhood Education: Insights and Issues*, B. Spodek and H. Walberg (eds.) (California: McCutchan Publishing Corp., 1977), pp. 116-137.

[3] R. W. Connell, *The Child's Construction of Politics* (Melbourne, Australia: Melbourne University Press, 1971).

[4] Robert Coles, "Children and Political Authority," in *The Mind's Fate* (Boston: Little, Brown, 1976), p. 252.

[5] Robert Coles, "Learning to Believe or Disbelieve in the American Dream," *Phi Delta Kappan* (September 1976).

[6] Lawrence Cremin, "Public Education and the Education of the Public," *Teachers College Record* 77:1

(September 1975): 5.

[7] Margery B. Franklin, and Barbara Biber, "Psychological Perspectives and Early Childhood Education: Some Relationships Between Theory and Practice," *Current Topics in Early Childhood Education,* Lillian G. Katz (ed.) (Ablex Publishing Corp., 1977), Vol. I; Barbara Biber, "Cognition in Early Childhood Education," Barbara Biber and Edna Shapiro, "The Education of Young Children: A Developmental Interaction Approach," *Teacher's College Record* 74 (September 1972);61-69; Patricia Minuchin, "Affective and Social Learning in the Early School Environment," in B. Spodek and H. J. Walbert, (eds.), *Early Childhood Education.*

[8] Barbara Biber and Edna Shapiro, "The Education of Young Children," pp. 61-69.

[9] R. W. Connell, *The Child's Construction of Politics.*

[10] Lewis Thomas, *Lives of a Cell* (New York: The Viking Press, 1974), p. 14.

[11] Don Edwards and Carol Polsgrove, "A Conversation with John Gardner," *Atlantic Monthly* 239:5 (May, 1977) p. 43.

[12] Barbara Biber and Edna Shapiro, "The Education of Young Children."

[13] Herbert Zimiles, "A Radical and Regressive Solution to the Problem of Evaluation," in Lillian G. Katz (ed.), *Current Topics in Early Childhood Education* (Ablex Publishing Corporation, 1977), Volume I.

[14] Robert Selman, "A Developmental Approach to Interpersonal and Moral Awareness in Young Children: Some Theoretical and Educational Implications of Levels of Perspective-Taking," in J. Meyer, B. Burnham, and Cholvat (eds.), *Value Education Theory, Practice, Problems and Prospects* (Waterloo, Ontario: W. Laurie Press, 1975), pp. 127-140.

[15] J. Piaget and A. Weil, *The Development in Children of the Idea of a Homeland and of Relations with other Countries,* International Social Science Bulletin 3 (1951): 561.

Additional Sources

Davison, Susan E. "Curriculum Materials and Resources for Law-Related Education," *Social Education* 41:3 (March 1977).

DeVries, R. and Kamii, C. *Why Group Games? A Piagetian Perspective,* ERIC Clearinghouse on Early Childhood Education. Urbana, Illinois: University of Illinois, 1976.

Easton, David and Dennis, Jack. *Children in the Political System, Origins of Political Legitimacy.* New York: McGraw-Hill Book Company, 1969.

Greenstein, Fred L. *Children and Politics.* New Haven: Yale University Press, 1965.

Hawley, Wills D. "Political Education and School Organization," *Theory into Practice* 10:5 (December 1971).

Hess, Robert D. and Torney, Judith V. *The Development of Political Attitudes in Children.* New York: Doubleday Anchor Book, 1968.

Jantz, Richard K. *"Social Studies" in Curriculum for the Preschool-Primary Child: A Review of the Research,* Carol Seefeldt (ed.). Columbus, Ohio: Charles E. Merrill Publishing Co., 1976.

Naylor, David. "Effective Training Programs for Elementary School Educators: Selected Issues and Recommendations." *Teaching Teachers about the Law.* Chicago: American Bar Association Youth Education for Citizenship, 1976.

Seefeldt, Carol. *Social Studies for the Preschool-Primary Child.* Columbus, Ohio: Charles E. Merrill Publishing Co., 1977.

Wyner, Nancy. "Another Species Endangered: The Young American Citizen. Thoughts and Comments on the Political and Legal Education of Primary School Children." ERIC ED 133275.

Wyner, Nancy. "Observations on the Teaching of Law in Elementary Schools." *Teaching Teachers about the Law.* Chicago, Illinois: American Bar Association Youth Education for Citizenship, September, 1976.

Figure 1

Guiding Principles for Curriculum and Teaching in Citizenship Education

Citizenship education

—Is specific—and therefore:

Provides children with accurate information on citizen-oriented matters

Involves children in active learning to help them develop democratic behaviors and gain knowledge and understanding of basic concepts and principles of American democracy

Provides learning activities that enable children to study the roles, responsibilities, careers, and human qualities of people in political life, and the organization, concerns, and problems of governance

—Is explicitly interrelated—and therefore:

Acknowledges the influences and resources of the child's environment

Integrates child development and the heritage of our political system—its broad underlying concepts and values—within the context of curriculum and instruction

Infuses democratic themes, values, and processes into the full range of the curriculm; i.e., reading, language arts, career, environmental and consumer education, art, and physical education

—Is person oriented—and therefore:

Considers the developmental capabilities and unique learning styles of individual students

Provides a setting in which adults seek to understand and respond to the child's perceptions, meanings, and actions

Underlines the influence and importance of key persons in the educational environment of the child (significantly the classroom teacher and school principal) in planning and supporting a democratically-oriented learning environment, exercising rationally-based authority, and providing a reasoned, consistent, and participatory approach to citizen development

Emphasizes the interdependence of people

—Is dynamically interactive—and therefore:

Stresses the interplay between the child and the social context, between the teacher and the child, and between children and the educative environment

Encourages children to use their full capacities in a school setting that nurtures cognition and social development, and that encourages personal and interpersonal growth and responsibility

Promotes instructional programs that are content- and process-oriented, that respond to individual and group needs, and that emphasize personal growth and social responsibility

Figure 2

Citizen Competencies Develop as the Child:

A. Engages in Thinking, Reasoning, and Social Interaction and:

B. Engages in Social/Political Interactions and:

Early Childhood

Begins to identify emotions in other people

Actively listens to what another person thinks, feels, intends

Collects accurate information and begins to organize it systematically

Communicates own viewpoint to another person and in a group context

Learns to take turns talking and listening, sharing, and helping

Shares ideas and feelings through language and symbolic representation

Clarifies misconceptions through questioning, observing, and comparing with accurate information

Recognizes that there is more than one point of view than his or her own, although they are assumed to be identical

Develops a personal sense of cooperation, participation, interdependence, sharing, and other pro-social behaviors

Communicates reasons for his or her ideas and feelings to others in a group context, or in one-to-one relationships

Understands the importance of having accurate information

Begins to understand that other people's thoughts and feelings are different from one's own

Recognizes that different people have different experiences, information, interests, and needs; yet acknowledges commonalities as well

Reflects on his or her own thoughts, feelings, and behavior

Early Childhood

Becomes aware of rules as a way of establishing boundaries, insuring personal safety, and protecting group life

Understands the need for rules, laws, and the processes for democratically making and changing rules/laws in the group life of the classroom, in local settings, and subsequently at the state and federal levels

Develops an increasing degree of personal freedom and self-discipline based on a reasoned approach to making choices and determining personal values

Is knowledgeable about symbols of national civic identity (e.g., flag, anthem, pledge) and is aware of national symbols of other world communities

Demonstrates increasing awareness and understanding of basic concepts of citizenship; for example, fairness, authority, participation, pluralism, freedom, governance, social responsibility, and interdependence

Participates in groups discussing social/political issues, developing a sense of competence about oneself as a member of groups

Is knowledgeable about roles and responsibilities of leaders and authorities

Demonstrates competencies in leadership roles among peers (planning, exercising fairness, and using democratic process—voting, majority rule, consensus, dissent)

Demonstrates increasing responsibility for achieving one's own rights and the rights and needs of others through the active application of knowledge, competencies, and personal values

Develops increasing base of knowledge, skills, attitudes to shape a sense of political self-concept

(Continued on next page)

Figure 2 (Continued)

Middle Childhood

Recognizes reciprocal influences that people have on each other's thoughts, feelings, and behavior

Can assume a viewpoint other than his or her own and views self from that vantage point, "putting self in someone else's shoes" and gaining a sense of the mutuality of roles

Demonstrates increasing awareness of the rights, needs, and feelings of self and others, and takes responsibility for promoting these rights, etc.

Participates cooperatively as a result of productive, satisfying group experiences and social collaboration

Can alter behavior to achieve and promote more effective interpersonal relationships

Middle Childhood

Distinguishes the political and governmental world from other areas of life and has knowledge of the general purpose and functions of government

Is conversant with major documents of our constitutional democracy (Bill of Rights, Constitution) and begins to compare their principles with the political orientation of other nations in the world—building toward a global perspective

Understands the facts and principles of our two-party political system and its importance in the growth of democracy

Is increasingly knowledgeable about citizen-oriented subject matter; for example, poverty, racism, environment protection, scarcity of resources, and conflict

Demonstrates a reasoned approach to conflict situations; applying negotiation, compromise, and due process, and can apply planning and advocacy techniques for constructive change

Shows ability to postpone immediate solutions in view of long-range consequences

---

Figure 3

Enabling Processes for Developing Citizen Competencies Include:

1. Group Discussion/Meetings

Teaching Decisions:

Setting appropriate limits and expectations for group participation

Selecting a time to hold meetings

Matching the length of meetings and discussions with attention span/interests of children

Choosing seating arrangements that increase communication and interaction

Selecting appropriate sources for discussion; i.e., children's experiences and current events

Determining when to intervene to guide the flow discussion, to help children focus, and to summarize

Student Actions:

Focusing on a theme, issue, idea, or problem

Listening to what another thinks, feels, or intends

Communicating views and sharing ideas

Formulating/responding to questions

Gathering accurate information

Learning to participate and cooperate with others

Interacting in a social situation

Increasing interpersonal competence

Broadening perspectives ("decentering")

(Continued on p. 54)

Figure 3 (Continued)

2. Role Taking

Selecting role-playing situations that relate to children's experiences

Selecting participants and "props" for staging the event and deepening student involvement

Debriefing the group to help children to expand and deepen learning. Debriefing involves questioning children to think about: (1) what was observed, (2) what information they gathered from these observations, (3) why the persons were acting as they did, and (4) how things might work out, and how they feel about it (valuing)

3. Field Trips

Teaching Decisions

Deciding on the purpose of the visit's goals for teaching/learning

Selecting and planning visits to settings in the community that are potentially stimulating and where people are interested, responsive, and concerned about learners

Deciding on means for recording the experience (e.g., cameras, tapes recorders, charts, and survey forms), drawings, and written reports

Discussing with children ways they can express their experiences—through role-play, murals, writing, photography

4. Gaming

Choosing the appropriate time and place

Clarifying the purpose of the game session

Choosing traditional, commercial, or student-developed games

Using the due-process format to help children resolve conflict through negotiation, compromise, and arbitration

Teaching participatory skills to make decisions, choose leaders and teams, and determine penalties and rewards (i.e., voting, majority rule, arbitration)

Exploring interactions with peers and dynamic alternatives by learning through reconstruction, re-enactment, and role taking

Cooperating to achieve a group goal

Suspending one's own viewpoint momentarily through role-shifting and finding out what it is like to be in the other person's shoes

Student Actions

Making firsthand observations of how the political environment operates, what government does, how elections are held, and what jobs people have

Collecting and organizing information about our political/social environment

Recording information for further discussions, research, and comparison

Studying vocabulary, reading books, and using visuals that contribute to and extend field-trip experiences

Interacting actively with peers and adult in the environment, and the consequent exposure to diverse places, people, life styles, and roles

Develops an awareness of boundaries rules, and conflict-provoking issues; and experiences a need for order and reason

Functions in situations in which adult authority is temporarily suspended, assuming responsibility for self

Develops skills in rule making, conflict resolution, and participation

Develops an experiential concept of self discipline

Understands the consequences of cheating and penalties

Coordinates skills and knowledge with others

Experiences the satisfaction of achieving common group goal

4
Children Parents, Teachers: Rediscovery of an Important Triad

Carol Cartwright

A significant trend in the movement of organized education is toward a closer coordination of the facilities of the home and of the school. If one were to inquire of any student of social progress, what is the newest development in the educational world, the answer would almost surely be, schools for infants and a constructive program of education for parents.[1]

Many people believe that the discovery of the importance of the early years and the home-school relationships that ought to exist for the facilitations of the child's development are recent phenomena. For them, it will be surprising to learn that the above statement does not come from a recent publication, but from the 1929 NSSE Yearbook on Preschool and Parental Education. Recognition of the need for programs to provide educational services for the child at an early age and also to provide for genuine involvement of the family in the school program is not something new. What *is* new within the past few years is a clearer understanding of the complexities involved in delivering a program of parent involvement. This knowledge is helpful to classroom teachers who seek informal interaction with parents and to those who are planning a more structured approach to parent involvement.

Parent Involvement

Currently many parents are expressing a desire for a more active involvement in their children's education. This comes at a time when there is increased societal concern for the continuation of the family as a social institution and when there is a new awareness of the complexity of the interaction between parents, educational institutions, and the broader society as they influence the growth and development of young children.

The idea of parent involvement in the education of children is one of several themes which are woven throughout the history of early childhood education in this country. Attitudes toward parents—their roles, their contributions, and programs and strategies proposed for involving them—vary among early childhood professionals. Positions range from one that views parent participation as vital for the successful development of the child to the view that parents have failed during the child's most formative years, thereby necessitating that social institutions intervene to facilitate the child's development.[2]

Renewed interest in the parent-teacher-child triad has been accompanied by new

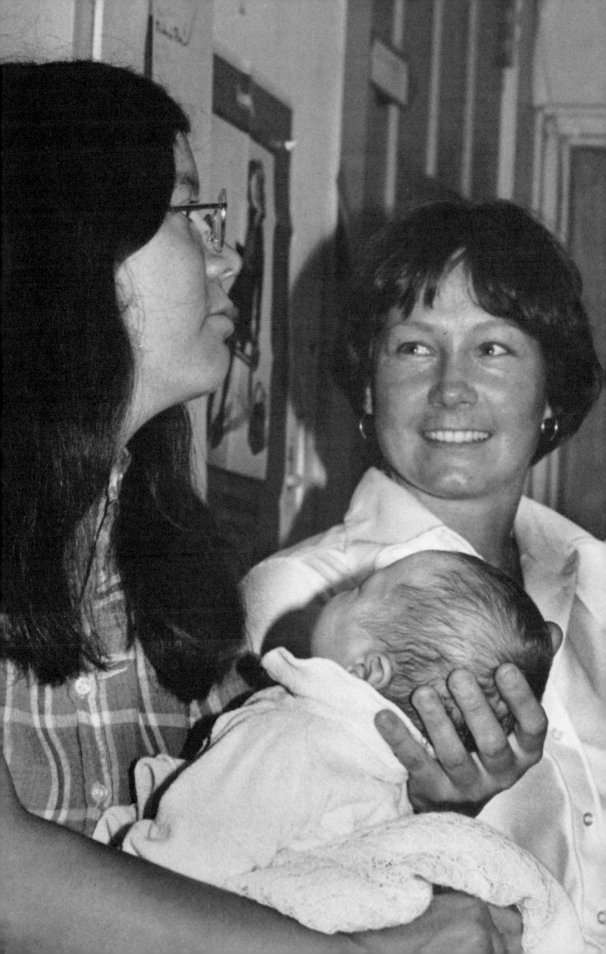

programs and new meanings for old terms. *Parent education* employs an educative process directed toward individuals or groups, the goal being to impart knowledge through a variety of methods and to use a number of disciplines with the expected result of positively changing the life of the family. *Parent involvement* is a broader term, referring to any effort to involve parents in programs and services primarily directed toward serving children. Classroom teachers tend to have more opportunities to relate to parents in terms of the more general aspect of parent involvement.

Parents and Social Studies

In this chapter, the focal group is expanded from children and teachers to include parents. The major goal of parent involvement is most often given as one that has educational benefit for the children, but the involvement process also results in benefits to parents and to society at large.[3]

The concept of parent involvement is relevant for social studies educators in two, quite different, ways. On the one hand, consider that parents have the initial and most continuous significant influence on their children. Those who work with young children must be convinced of the value of parent involvement and need to explore means of working with parents. There is a knowledge base for parent involvement, and it should be used when seeking answers to the question "How can teachers and parents work together?"

At a different level, topics associated with parent involvement are appropriate components of the curriculum for social studies at all age levels. Early childhood educators have long recognized that much of the content of programs for young children is primarily social education, and they have integrated the concepts of social education and social skills with traditional early education activities. These educators recognize the need to weave ideas about home and family life into the curriculum. Further, they understand the need to intervene in children's social interactions to encourage the development of positive feelings about self and family. Within the developmental-interactionist view, there are important goals for young children which are dependent for their full achievement upon the involvement of parents. Among these goals are: helping children deal with conflicts; encouraging the development of self-image; and assisting children to establish mutually supporting patterns of interaction.[4]

Aspects of family life should be integral components of the social studies curriculum for intermediate-grade children and adolescents, just as they are for younger children. Beatrice Paolucci and Stanley Wronski state: "Serious and substantive inquiry into the study of the family can be critical to illuminating the human condition and influencing the future of humanity.... Social educators will be continuously involved not only in developing practical courses in family life education, but will be equally concerned with understanding the interplay of family with other institutions in an effort to create social, economic, and philosophical environments that will illuminate the human condition.... The study of the family has never loomed as important or as challenging as it does today. The role of social educators is primarily one of helping students acquire a vision of what the family *is*, what it *is becoming*, and what it *could be*."[5]

Social studies education involves the study of attitudes and values as well as content from history, geography, and other disciplines. Attitudes and values toward the role of the family in American society are important aspects of the development of citizenship. It has been said, "The basic justification for teaching social studies is the contribution it can make to an individual's potential for acting wisely in human affairs."[6] Because citizens must make decisions about human resources as well as material resources, the study of the status and role of the family, the parenting process, and the impact of pluralistic family patterns must be components of the social studies curriculum throughout the school experience.

Importance of Parent Involvement

State of the Family

The National Council of Organizations for Children and Youth recently prepared a factbook about American families that contains a wealth of statistical data concerning children in poverty, child health problems, changes in American family structure, child care needs, and federal programs serving children.[7] The overriding conclusion drawn from the factbook is that all is far from well for America's children and families. Many problems can be traced to the general lack of public policies advocating a better life for families. Consideration of the problems faced by American families constitutes part of the rationale for parent involvement. These problems include: the diversity and confusion apparent in society about child-rearing practices; the extent of child abuse and neglect; an inadequate health care system; the poor environments in which children grow up, which are hostile because of slums, pollution, and crime; the rapid increase of mothers in the work force; general distrust of institutions among the citizenry; poor attitudes towards the schools; and, finally, the absence of professional help for parents in rearing their children.[8] Lane stated that "The single most important function of life—the development of human beings—has been left out of the educational curriculum."[9]

Significant changes in the structure of the American family have been documented. In 1975, 36 per cent of the children under six years of age had mothers in the labor force.[10] One out of every six children under the age of 18 now lives with only one parent.[11] The existence of these conditions suggests a need for programs to help families in stress to deal with parenthood.

The preparation and continuous professional development of classroom teachers in their own social education are also considerations. Teachers who are aware of conditions in the home and of the general anxieties and stresses of parenting, and who are sensitive to the diversity of values and beliefs about children among parents, may be more successful in involving parents in school programs.

Lack of Preparation for Parenthood

When one considers the enormous stakes in the parenting process, it would seem that responsibilities for parenthood would not be taken lightly or left to chance. Usually people have some training for important roles in life—their jobs, for example—but seldom do people receive training for the role of parents. Folklore about parenting may affect adults' behavior, and "they are apt to think their behavior is based on sound rational principles when in reality it is not."[12] The message from many researchers and authors currently working in the field is that parenting is a learning and growing process.[13] More and more, we are considering the adult development aspects of parent involvement.

Parents Are the Child's First Teachers

Parenting involves a teaching responsibility. The idea that parents are the child's first teachers is a key aspect of the rationale for parent involvement. While we have long acknowledged the teaching functions of parents, the following passage captures the essence of this parental teaching role as understood today:

> What is new is our understanding that the way in which we teach has a pervasive effect, not just on what children learn, but on how they learn to view their experience and how to use it. In other words, in their learning how to learn. These learnings are not the result of didactic teaching, but are implicit in the content of daily interacting between parent and child. Whether or not the parent is aware of this process, by the simple act of becoming a parent, he suddenly takes on a totally new function, the task of teaching.[14]

There is wide agreement that the teaching role of parents is crucial for the optimal development of the child. Most parents have a need to better understand and execute their teaching functions.

Children Perform Better When Parents Are Involved

Some educators stress that parents have a basic human right to be involved in their child's education.[15] Others are more persuaded by empirical evidence which supports the idea that children, on the average, do better in the educational program when the parents are somehow involved in the proc-

ess.[16] Some of the evidence has been so persuasive that the federal government has mandated parent involvement in programs such as Head Start, Follow Through, and Title XX Day Care.

Benefits to Society

Together with the evidence that parent involvement benefits children is the belief that parent involvement efforts will benefit society at large because of the improved contributions that both parents and children will make to the larger community. Bronfenbrenner states: ". . . the involvement of the parents as partners in the enterprise provides an ongoing system which can reinforce the effects of the program while it is in operation and help to sustain them after the program ends."[17]

There is a reciprocity in regard to the impact of improved parenting on the community. Among others, Grams emphasizes that parenting is not confined to parents but is a function ". . . shared by all individuals and organizations of individuals concerned with the development of children."[18]

The Impact of a Changing World and Cultural Pluralism

The impact of the rapid pace of societal change in recent years is a concern. Today's parents are expected (with or without help) to prepare their children for a world that they themselves have never known. Because of rapid changes in society, it is no longer possible to rely on tradition to guide parenting behavior.

The cultural pluralism that characterizes much of our life is relevant for those working with parents. There is diversity in the goals of parents and in their attitudes toward child rearing, family life, and schooling which must be recognized and respected. Cultural diversity is a positive aspect of our society and ought to be encouraged, rather than thwarted. Classroom teachers can modify their approaches, so parent involvement is consistent with diverse family life styles and attitudes and yet still beneficial to the children and families.

Types of Parent Involvement

Parents can be seen as complaining, illiterate, lazy, unconcerned, over-worked, and hostile; but they can also be seen as consumers, learners, models, aides, resources, volunteers, observers, teachers, and policy-makers. The attitude of teachers and program planners toward parents will influence the design of the program, its orientation, and the roles parents assume in their involvement.[19]

Assumptions About Family Problems

Different models for parental involvement and for intervention with children and parents have implicit and explicit assumptions about the family. Recognition of the assumptions and their impact on the nature of parent involvement is important for teachers because, to be most effective, strategies for parent involvement must be in agreement with belief systems.

The *deficit* intervention model is based on the idea that the child has missed out on many experiences which are available to the middle class, causing a cumulative deficit phenomenon with increasing age. Assuming child deficiencies, the educational program for both children and parents is remedial in nature. A contrasting view is found in the *school-as-failure* model, in which the problem is seen as residing in the school system, rather than in the family. This orientation implies retraining of teachers, redesigning of the curriculum, and improved mutual communication between the home and the school. When this model is operating, parents are more often viewed as resources and decision-makers.

A third view is the *cultural difference* model, in which it is assumed that the child has had learning experiences but that they differ from those of the general culture. This view, which supports cultural pluralism, involves adapting the curriculum of the school and using the parents as resources and teachers in the school. Yet another view, the *social*

structural model, is related to general social processes. In this view, individuals' behaviors will be related to such factors as their status in the social structure, the positions they occupy, and the demands and expectations that society places on them. Programs in this model tend to be more concerned with community issues and policies to change social structures than with individual children or families. Parents as policy-makers would be an essential component of this model.

Roles for Parents

Roles parents play in early education programs appear to fall along a continuum ranging from nominal to extensive and genuine parent involvement.[20] Listed in order from least to most involvement, these roles are as follows:

1. Parents as supporters, service givers, and facilitators
2. Parents as learners
3. Parents as teachers of their own children
4. Parents as teacher aides and volunteers in the classroom
5. Parents as policy-makers and partners.

Parents as *supporters* occupy the lowest position on the involvement continuum. These parents may work in fund raising, babysitting, or food service programs. These parents are most often observers or bystanders, since they are essentially uninvolved in whatever directly affects their children's learning. The purpose for involving parents as *learners* is to improve parents' knowledge and skills so that they can do a better job of child rearing. The teacher is viewed as the expert, and the parent is seen as deficient in the necessary skills for parenting. The midpoint on the involvement continuum is the role for parents as *teachers* of their own children, often in the home. Parents, usually mothers, are taught various ways of enhancing cognitive development and managing behavior. This parent role can be viewed both positively and negatively in that parents are seen as deficient in the skills to teach their own children, but are later seen as adequate teachers once they have been prepared by the experts. Parents may also serve as *paid aides* or as *volunteers* in the classroom.

The role for parents which represents the most genuine involvement is that of parents as *policy-makers* and *partners*. These parents may be involved in planning, operation, and evaluation of programs. In Head Start, Follow Through, The Parent-Child Center programs, and some day-care programs, parent participation in policy-making is required.

Schools, Teachers, and Parent Involvement

School programs are crucial and fundamental components upon which genuine and effective parent involvement is based.[21] From a practical point of view, the school is often considered a meeting ground between parents and teachers. Both teachers and parents are assumed to share mutual concerns about the enhancement of children's development and learning. Both want to provide opportunities from which children can benefit as much as possible in living, learning, and growing. The importance of the school as a common meeting place for parents and teachers to share mutual concerns is recognized through parent-involvement programs.

In a democratic society, the objectives of the school are supposed to be products derived from parent and teacher participation. Parents and teachers working together augment the educational efforts of the schools, and, in turn, the home and school as institutions become strengthened through recognition of commonly generated and mutually relevant goals.[22] The environments of home and school are both contributing forces that shape the child. A democratic atmosphere which supports and challenges children's responding and decision-making is thought to facilitate the acquisition of adaptive behaviors. The similarities between parenting and teaching in style, environment, and democratic atmosphere are evidence of the need for the schools and parents to work together.

Delivery Systems

The method of planning parent programs to develop and expand parent involvement should be carefully considered. The delivery system for parent involvement may, in part, determine success or failure. Rushing into parent involvement on a district-wide basis or mandating parent involvement in one or two classrooms or in an entire school is inappropriate. With recognition of the importance of parent involvement to the school, the parents, and the children, careful study and coordination is required prior to formal program implementation. Budgetary commitment, human and material resources available, and the desired method of implementing parent involvement require consideration. Approaches to parent involvement should be carefully explored in a precise and systematic manner and in the context of resources available. Methods of implementing parent-involvement programs are related to delivery systems or to the ways in which parents, teachers, and children come together to work with one another. These delivery systems include: (1) school-based programs, (2) home-based programs, and (3) combination approaches including both home and school components.

School-based programs. School-based parent-involvement programs usually require the parent to come to the school or early childhood center. Training procedures, parent-teacher interaction, and adult-child work all occur in the school. Advantages of a school-based delivery system are the ease of training (because all equipment and materials are readily available) and the increased communication among parents (because parents have the opportunity of talking and working with many other parents). Parents are able to see development take place with many children over long and short periods of time.

A notable parenting project for adolescents was recently instituted in some schools. It is the education for parenthood approach which has a preventive emphasis. The curriculum generally includes information about child development and socialization and practical experiences with young children. One such curriculum, "Exploring Childhood," is a one-year elective course for 7th through 12th graders, and has been field tested and is now being disseminated nationwide.[23] In addition to information about child development, family functioning, and child rearing, students are helped to identify their own values and beliefs about children and parenthood.

Home-based programs. Home-based parent-involvement programs rely heavily upon school personnel working as parent educators to achieve educational objectives by indirectly working with youngsters through their parents. Classroom teachers are rarely involved in this approach. Parents are the direct teaching interface with the child. Generally, professional educators travel to the home, and all training and interaction take place exclusively in home environments. This particular delivery system has some advantages. Especially for young children, the home setting is often preferred.[24] It may also be an ideal way to serve handicapped youngsters who vary in exceptionality and levels of functioning.[25] This approach implicitly recognizes the crucial role of parents as the most important and continuous developmental influence in their children's lives.

Combination Approach. Some parent-involvement programs combine the school and home as delivery systems. With this type of parent-involvement program, interaction between the parent, teacher, and child can take place in either home or school settings. The individual advantages of both systems can be exploited, but systematic planning is required to coordinate the program.

Common Program Components

Regardless of delivery systems chosen by the school or the community agency, there are several common program elements. After decisions about the type of delivery system, the specific program components must be systematically planned and developed. Program components fundamental to all delivery systems are: rationale, intake and screening, service delivery, liaison and follow through, and evaluation.[26]

The rationale includes a plan for administrative organization of the program and a clearly defined statement of goals. Intake and screening procedures used in identifying and selecting the parents for the program must be determined in advance. The service delivery component defines the resources used in implementing and operationalizing the program. These resources include types and kinds of parent-training procedures, materials used in the training, and planned practice sessions with professional and parent educa-

tor modeling teaching routines. Liaison and follow-through components provide opportunities for parents to be involved in work sessions with teachers and children. These sessions will indicate whether or not the training and involvement activities are affecting parents' behaviors and children's learning.

The evaluation component should be designed to assess the effect of the entire parent-involvement program. Typical questions about the program that should be asked are: (1) What has the program accomplished over the period of time it was in operation? (2) How has the program accomplished its stated objectives? (3) What areas of the program need improvement? Evaluation of effectiveness and efficiency will be helpful in planning for the future.

Notable Parent-Involvement Projects

The momentum of the early efforts in parent involvement was lost during World War II and was not really regained until the 1960s. Whereas earlier, parent involvement generally meant the passive receiving of child development information and the mutual sharing of concerns about child rearing, since Head Start and other federal efforts in the 1960s the ideas about parent programs are considerably broader. Parent participation and parent involvement are now important concepts.[27] Several projects frequently cited in the literature as models are briefly described in the next section. These models serve as a rich resource for any classroom teacher or school administrator interested in developing better working relationships with parents.

Head Start

From its inception in 1965, Head Start included an expressed aim for parent involvement for "the improvement of the parent's self-esteem and self-worth to the point where he [or she] can take his [or her] place in the community as an informed and participating adult and become an advocate of education."[28] Parent involvement is still a vital component of Head Start programs. In fact, it is a required condition for federal funding. The effects of the parent involvement component as implemented in various Head Start programs have been documented and results are generally positive.[29] The objectives of all Head Start programs are directed at improving: (1) the child's physical health and physical skills; (2) the emotional and social development of the child; (3) the child's cognitive processes and skills; (4) the child's relationships among the family and simultaneously strengthening the family's ability to relate to the child; (6) the child's and the family's attitudes toward society; and (7) the child's and the family's sense of dignity and self-worth.[30]

The majority of studies about the impact of Head Start on families report, "an improvement in parenting abilities as well as a satisfaction with the educational gains of their children."[31] With regard to parents' behaviors, the researchers report, "an increase in positive interactions between mothers and their children, as well as an increase in parent participation in later school programs."[32] Success with the parent involvement component of Head Start spurred the development of several model programs which were primarily based on the participation of parents as either teachers or policymakers, or both.

Home Start

Home Start, a federal effort initiated in 1972, was designed to meet the needs of families without access to Head Start programs by providing Head Start types of programs which were home-based rather than center-based. Sixteen demonstration programs were initially funded to serve 2,500 children.[33]

Home Start projects were designed to use existing community resources and services. Parents represent only one component of the program in Head Start, but they are the *major* component of Home Start. A basic notion underlying Home Start was that parents could be taught to effectively help their children at home to do the same things teachers were doing in Head Start classes. Thus, Home Start Training Centers provide field-based training in areas such as the role and skills of the home visitor; enhancing the role of parents; and selection, development, and use of curricular materials.

The results of a recent national evaluation of the original 16 Home Start projects are supportive of this approach to achieve goals similar to those of Head Start programs.[34] Of special interest to those involved in implementing home-based programs are the following conclusions: (1) Home visit frequency was affected by program location and focal child age. (2) Variations in the frequency and duration of home visits had an effect on both parent and child outcomes.[35]

Perry Preschool Project

The Perry Preschool Project, initiated in Ypsilanti, Michigan in 1962, is a model approach involving both home and school as sites for delivering services. The project included a classroom program for children with a curriculum based on Piagetian theory. A home-teaching program was also a major project component. Goals for parents included: becoming oriented to the teaching as well as to the disciplinary functions of the parent-child interaction; adopting a teaching style that could be expected to reinforce the child's growth; knowing how to obtain necessary information about the child's developmental levels so that teaching would be appropriately pitched; and knowing how to support and encourage the child's language development. A program coordinator was responsible for arranging home visits, and classroom teachers were responsible for carrying out the visits to the parents in the homes. Parents were encouraged to participate as volunteers in the classes. In general, research results of these programs indicate that the approach is a viable one for teaching parents to help their children make developmental progress.[36]

Florida Parent Education Program

The unique aspect of the program developed at the University of Florida under the leadership of Ira Gordon is that paraprofessionals are trained to be parent educators for their parent peers. The model is based on the assumption that parents are adequate as teachers of their children, and program activities are designed to enhance this already existing basic teaching adequacy. Specific goals for parents include: (1) increasing parents' abilities to teach their own children;

(2) improving parents' feelings of interpersonal adequacy; (3) increasing parental attendance and participation in school-based activities; (4) increasing parents' skills in relating with the school; (5) increasing the time that parents spend with their children in educational and recreational activities; and (6) improving the feelings of control that parents have over their own lives.[37] A five-week training program for the parent educators, who are usually women from the same socioeconomic level as the target parents, is included. In the homes, they present specific tasks for the parents to learn through a combination of role playing and demonstration. Diffusion of information is expected when target mothers share their new competencies informally with neighbors. Research suggests that the program had value for children's development and that parents had a better image of themselves as teachers and were more committed to continuing participation in their children's education.[38]

Selected General Strategies for Genuine Parent Involvement

As noted earlier, there are a number of roles for participants in parent involvement programs, and some roles involve more genuine participation than others. The active roles for parents involve them directly in the operation of the school program. This is social education in action. When roles are active, parents do more than attend teacher conferences to discuss their child's achievement or passively receive school newsletters and handouts describing the operation of the program. Parents become actively involved with teaching children and play a more causal role in helping shape the educational objectives of the schools. These points of emphasis provide a general framework within which to place the strategies and principles fundamental to genuine parent involvement in educational programs.

Professionals currently working in parent-involvement programs have produced a number of general suggestions. These include:

1. Parents must develop an understanding of themselves as individuals involved in the educative process;

2. Parents must acquire basic knowledge of the child's development;

3. Open communication patterns between and among parents, teachers, and children must be understood and practiced.

These areas of involvement can be enhanced through interaction, observation of children, and communication.

Interacting

Adults in a program of training and parent involvement must have the opportunity to explore and evaluate their self-concepts, as well as other aspects of personality. This helps solidify what they understand and believe about working with children and functioning as parents. Parents can be helped to recognize their personal aspirations for achievement for their child. They can learn to assess the physical and psychological means that they provide for their child's needs. Exploring selected social and emotional areas also assists in reducing guilt feelings and feelings of inadequacy that parents may have about themselves as individuals, or about methods they use in rearing their children. The opportunity for exploration provides participants with socially stimulating activities and experiences in informal group meetings. A process of open, informal discussions using an activity format has the potential of increasing positive feelings about the parenting processes, the family structure, children, and themselves as parents and teachers.

With increased personal understanding, parents have greater awareness of the child's self-concept and can find constructive ways of assisting the youngster's acquisition of positive attitudes. For example, when parents participate as volunteers in the classroom they can convey to their children the idea that school is an interesting and exciting place by walking to school with their children, animatedly discussing the events planned for the day, and encouraging follow-up discussion about their involvement with their children later in the evening. In this way, parents provide their children with a model of positive participation in the schools.

For individuals to explore self-concept and

other related aspects of personality, it is important that an atmosphere of acceptance and trust be developed within the parent group. In small group settings of three to five parents, the staff leader and the group can safely explore understandings, feelings, attitudes, and beliefs about themselves and their work with children in an informal and nonthreatening manner. It is essential that group leaders have adequate skills in group facilitation, an understanding of the influence of individual family background on the discussion, and a sensitivity and ability to encourage goals that emerge from the group. With supportive group leadership, interacting behavior can be further defined, topics of interest to the parents can be discussed, and needed teaching strategies can be demonstrated, modeled, and practiced.

Observing

Developing parent-involvement programs requires much attention to and practice in observing young children's behavioral patterns. By observing what young children do and say and how they behave, parents can achieve a better understanding of the child's level of learning and can acquire concepts of developmental change. They can be taught to compare observations made on specific children across various time intervals. Through the process of acquiring a series of baseline observations of the same children over varied time periods, parents can isolate verbal, motor, and nonverbal behaviors of the young child and learn to recognize developmental changes in growth and learning. Help from the professional educator is needed to guide the participants in what to observe and how to observe. Observation techniques are described in Chapter One.

Observation coupled with informal group discussion can produce important insight into changes in behavioral repertoires. Discovering and unlocking behavioral patterns of young children can facilitate cooperation and group effort between members of the parent group. Parents can also observe and record children's behaviors at home as a means of documenting child growth and program effectiveness.

When behaviors which are easily described and observed are the focus of jointly designed and conducted parent-teacher observational projects, parents are able to take an active role in observing and record keeping. When the change projects occur over a long period of time and when parents are involved in the record-keeping aspects of the project, they can see tangible results of their involvement with their children. For example, if parent and teacher decided that a child needed help in controlling verbal outbursts of temper when adults requested that a task be completed, the parents could be responsible for the home and the teacher for the school aspects of the change project. The goal of decreasing the number of verbal outbursts could be managed and documented at home by parents, and, at certain regularly scheduled conferences, parent and teacher could compare their records and discuss progress over time in both home and school settings. The parent and teacher would have agreed at the beginning of the project about definitions of appropriate responses to adult requests, about the techniques to be used to effect change, and about the type of recording to be used. Since the parent would have the same responsibilities as the teacher, the parent would be able to function as a real partner in the project. Classroom teachers can initiate these techniques on an individual basis or within the structures of a formal parent involvement program.

Communicating

Developing ways to effectively communicate information about the program, child, parent, and teacher is an overriding concern of parent involvement programs. The outcome of facilitating communication is a clearer understanding of the mutuality of goals and objectives between home and center or school and more thorough definitions of the roles of parent and professional educators. In the context of parent involvement programs, the basic components of the communication process are: (1) learning to share; (2) learning to listen; and (3) learning to work together.[39]

Encouraging parents and teachers to share thoughts and feelings provides a forum to discuss attitudes and beliefs about teaching strategies and child-rearing practices, and it develops open lines of communication. Ideas

and attitudes presented by group members help establish a climate of acceptance, as well as the recognition that there are many common views and similar perspectives among group members. Parents can practice listening skills by listening to children as they go about their day-to-day activities. Being attentive to verbal and nonverbal cues, parents can learn much about adults and children and their relationships to others. Body and facial movements, voice tones, and other indicators provide additional sources that can help to explain real meanings behind words. Learning to identify nonverbal and verbal behaviors and interpreting them in context become real assets for parents.

Helping parents develop problem-solving abilities (and parents, in turn, helping children) is another fundamental component of effective communication. When parents and children learn to work together, decisions can be made and problems solved. Hasty answers can be questioned, and more time can be given to participation in decision-making. Parent educators can model ways of exploring alternatives and weighing predictable consequences of behaviors. Even though children vary in developmental abilities, each youngster can be given opportunities to demonstrate and practice decision-making. It is only through practice that the child is eventually able to deal with more complex problems and issues.

A positive approach to parent involvement rests on the assumption that parents generally wish to do a better job of parenting. It follows, then, that every effort should be made to involve parents in identifying and solving their own problems. It is a widely accepted notion that genuine involvement in decision-making results in greater possibilities for real change and more lasting solutions. If we believe that parents want to be good parents, we need to encourage parent involvement beginning early in the life of the child.

Closing Comments

Programs designed to deliver services directly to children and families are multiplying rapidly, as is the research effort aimed at documenting the effectiveness of programs and strategies for parent involvement. Professionals interested in program implementation, basic and applied researchers, and public policy-makers are all talking about parents. Several important public policy papers have recently been published, and they point to the need for a public policy which supports families to achieve a better life for children in the United States.[40] The thrust of most of these position statements is that public responsibility does not necessarily translate into public care.[41]

In 1972, the Carnegie Corporation created the Carnegie Council on Children. The purpose of the Council is to work on problems of children and families in this country. The work of the Council will no doubt be widely disseminated and discussed in the next decade. Several books describing the work of the Council and the conclusions reached by those on the Council have already been published, and additional volumes anticipated shortly. The work which is most relevant for the topic being discussed here is entitled *All Our Children: The American Family Under Pressure*, by Keniston.[42] Its central thesis is that American families can never be thought of as separate from the society within which they function. The realities of life in this day and age in America do not mesh well with the myths and folklore about the roles and functions of families. The implications for public policy-makers are that children cannot be dealt with in isolation from families; and, in turn, families cannot be dealt with in isolation from society at large. The current expectations for families are presented as un-realistic. For example, ". . .the parent today is usually a coordinator without a voice or authority, a maestro trying to conduct an orchestra of players who have never met and who play from a multitude of different scores, each in a notation the conductor cannot read. If parents are frustrated it is no wonder; for although they have the responsibility for their children's lives, they hardly ever have the voice, the authority, or the power to make others listen to them."[43] The arguments are compelling; the solution which is proposed by the Council will be controversial. In essence, the proposal says that the only way to support the future generation is to support families now.

As Keniston voiced the concerns of the Council, "The society we imagine would be one that put children first, not last, that set the development of a vital, resourceful, caring, moral generation of Americans as the nation's highest priority. The devotion that individual parents now feel to their own children would be broadened to include everyone's children. The next generation's strength and well-being would become everyone's responsibility."[44] Keniston is surely voicing the concerns of most of us, since he is really talking about the development of a concerned citizenry, a major goal of social studies education.

Footnotes

[1] National Society for the Study of Education, *Preschool and Parent Education* (Bloomington, Illinois: Public School Publishing Company, 1929).

[2] L. Datta, *Parent Involvement in Early Childhood Education: A Perspective from the United States* (Washington, D.C.: N.I.E., 1973), ERIC ED 088 587; E. Grotberg, "Institutional Responsibilities for Early Childhood Education," in *Early Childhood Education: The Seventy-first Yearbook of the National Society for the Study of Education*, ed. I. J. Gordon (Chicago, Illinois: University of Chicago Press, 1972), pp. 317-388; M. Lazerson, "The Historical Antecedents of Early Childhood Education," *ibid.*, pp. 33-53.

[3] C. S. Chilman, "Programs for Disadvantaged Parents," in *Review of Child Development Research* (Chicago, Illinois: University of Chicago Press, 1973), Vol. 3, pp. 403-465; E. Pickarts and J. Fargo, *Parent Education: Toward Parental Competence* (New York: Appleton-Century-Crofts, 1971).

[4] B. Biber, E. Shapiro, and D. Wickens, *Promoting Cognitive Growth: A Developmental Interaction Point of View* (Washington, D. C.: National Association for the Education of Young Children, 1971).

[5] B. Paolucci and S. P. Wronski, "The American Family and Social Education," *Social Education* 41:6 (1977): 470-471.

[6] J. R. Lee, *Teaching Social Studies in the Elementary*

School (New York: Free Press, 1974).

[7] *America's Children 1976: A Bicentennial Assessment* (Washington, D. C.: National Council of Organizations for Children and Youth, 1976).

[8] *Ibid;* General Mills, Inc., *Raising Children in a Changing Society* (Minneapolis, Minn.: General Mills, Inc., 1977).

[9] M. B. Lane, *Education for Parenting* (Washington, D.C.: National Association for the Education of Young Children, 1975), p. 4.

[10] *America's Children 1976.* NCOCY.

[11] *Ibid.*

[12] E. E. Le Masters, *Parents in Modern America*, rev. ed. (Homewood, Illinois: Dorsey Press, 1974), pp. 19-30.

[13] F. Dodson, *How to Parent* (Bergenfield, New Jersey: New American Library, Inc., 1970), T. B. Brazelton, *Toddlers and Parents* (New York: Dell Publishing Co., 1974); B. Fisher and R. L. Fisher, *What We Really Know about Child Rearing* (New York: Basic Books, 1976).

[14] Pickarts and Fargo, *Parent Education*, p. 6.

[15] A. S. Honig, *Parent Involvement in Early Childhood Education* (Washington, D.C.: National Association for the Education of Young Children, 1975).

[16] I. J. Gordon, *Parent Involvement in Compensatory Education* (Urbana, Illinois: University of Illinois Press, 1970).

[17] U. Bronfenbrenner, *Is Early Intervention Effective: A Report on Longitudinal Evaluations of Preschool Programs*, Volume II (Washington, D.C.: OCD, HEW, 1974), p. 55.

[18] A. Grams, *Parenting: Concept and Process*, in Markum, (Ed.), *Parenting* (Washington, D.C.; Association for Childhood Education International, 1973), p 1.

[19] R. Hess, M. Block, J. Costello, R. Knowles, and D. Largay, "Parent Involvement in Early Education," in E. Grotberg (Ed.), *Day Care: Resources for Decision* (Washington, D.C.: OCD, HEW, 1971).

[20] *Ibid.*; I. J. Gordon, "Developing Parent Power," in Grotberg (Ed.), *Critical Issues in Research Relating to Disadvantaged Children* (Princeton, New Jersey: Educational Testing Service, 1969).

[21] Honig, *Parent Involvement in Early Childhood Education*, 1975.

[22] *Ibid.*

[23] S. Kruger, "Education for Parenthood and School-age Parents," *Journal of School Health*, 45 (1975): 292-295.

[24] D. L. Lillie, "Dimensions in Parent Programs: An Overview," in J. Grim, (Ed.), *Training Parents to Teach* (Chapel Hill, N.C.: Technical Assistance Development Center, Frank Porter Graham Child Development Center, 1968), p. 1-9.

[25] M. S. Shearer, "A Home-based Parent Training Model," in J. Grim, *Training Parents to Teach*, pp. 49-62.

[26] D. L. Lillie, "Dimensions in Parent Programs," pp. 1-9.

[27] L. Datta, *Parent Involvement in Early Childhood Education*, 1973.

[28] D. Phelps, "Project Headstart: A Professional Challenge," *Adult Leadership*, 15 (1966): 41-42.

[29] A. J. Mann, A. Harrell, and M. Hurt, *Review of Head Start Research Since 1969 and an Annotated Bibliography* (Washington, D. C.: DHEW Publication No. 77-31102 1977).

[30] *Ibid.*

[31] *Ibid.*

[32] *Ibid.*

[33] R. O'Keefe, "How About Home as a Place to Start?", *Urban Review*, 6 (1973): 35-37.

[34] J. M. Love, M. J. Nauta, C. G. Coelen and others. *National Home Start Evaluation: Final Report* (Ypsilanti, Michigan: High/Scope Educational Research Foundation, and Cambridge, Massachusetts: Abt Associates, Inc., 1977), pp. 14-20.

[35] *Ibid.*, p. 25.

[36] D. Weikart (Ed.), *Preschool Intervention: A Preliminary Report of the Preschool Project* (Ann Arbor, Michigan: Campus Publishers, 1967).

[37] I. J. Gordon, G. Greenwood, W. Ware, and P. Olmstead, *The Florida Parent Education Follow Through Program* (Gainesville, Florida: University of Florida, 1974).

[38] *Ibid.*

[39] T. D. Yawkey and L. Bakawa-Evenson, "The Child Care Professional, Parent, Child: An Emerging Triad," *Child Care Quarterly*, 4:3 (1975): 172-179.

[40] B. Greenblatt, *Responsibility for Child Care* (San Francisco, California: Jossey-Bass, 1977); K. S. Goldman and M. Lewis, *Child Care and Public Policy: A Case Study* (Princeton, New Jersey: Educational Testing Service, 1976); National Academy of Sciences, *Toward a National Policy for Children and Families* (Washington, D.C.: National Academy of Sciences, 1976); G. Y. Steiner, *The Children's Cause* (Washington, D.C.: The Brookings Institutions, 1976).

[41] *Ibid.*

[42] K. Keniston and Carnegie Council on Children, *All Our Children* (New York: Harcourt, Brace, Jovanovich, 1977).

[43] *Ibid.*, p. 18.

[44] *Ibid.*, pp. 220-221.

5
Children and Media
Luberta Mays and Alicia L. Pagano

One of the outstanding environmental changes of the twentieth century has been the innovations in media. Mass communications and telecommunications have transformed the world and what people see and hear. This assault on the various senses through media has brought about a radical reconstruction of people's auditory and visual experiences and has affected the way people perceive and learn about the world.

The availability of a variety of multimedia hardware for use by teachers and children in the classroom and outside classes has led to the development of new approaches for teaching young children. In this chapter we will consider some procedures for using television and other forms of media as aids to the social education of young children. We will describe methods which give children the greatest opportunity to interact within their environments.

Television

Television has profoundly affected the way in which members of the human race learn to become human beings.[1]

This statement by George Gerbner, Dean of the School of Communications at the University of Pennsylvania, reflects the extensive influence of television upon society. In Chapter Three, Nancy Wyner asks a recurring question about the varieties of experiences in America. "What common experiences bind America together toward a sense of national identity and citizenship in this multicultural and diverse nation?" It often seems as if *television is the one common experience that all American children now share.* A study prepared for the National Science Foundation reports, "It is clear that watching television is a nearly universal experience for children growing up in this country."[2] Rich or poor, urban or suburban, East or West, North or South, recent immigrant or Native American—most people view television; all have similar program options.

The educational possibilities for television in the future are even greater than those of today. The technologies are now available (and some are already in use) for interactive programming, world-stage telecasting via satellites, cable television, pay television, games attached to the picture tube, programmed learning wired through telephone and television, and the capabilities for 1000 channels of programming. These advances, and many others, are certain to result in more extensive uses of this medium than anyone would have thought possible a few short years ago.

Television has taken on a major and permanent role in classroom instruction and in learning outside of school. It is a medium with which all children identify and which all educators must regard as a teaching tool. Current television technology needs to be explored and utilized by educators at every level of childhood learning in order to maximize its potential as a positive means to affect the mental and social growth of young children.

Children's Viewing

Recent research of the use of television in America provides the following findings about television and viewing patterns by children under the age of 12.

1. Availability of television:
   —4% of American homes had television in 1948
   —90% of American homes had television in 1958
   —97% of homes had one television set, and 43% had more than one set in 1975[3]
   Thus, television is readily available to most American children.
2. Amount of time children watch television:
   —14% of American children regularly use television by age two, 37% by age three, 65% by age four, and 91% by age six[4]
   —Average child under 12 spends approximately 25 hours per week watching television[5]
   —The above figures were collected during the last two decades, and from these dated statistics we can conclude that "a majority of children are watching television regularly before age four.[6]
3. Viewing patterns of children:
   —Children under 12 spend 85% of their viewing time watching non-children's programs and only 15% watching programs designed for children.[7]
   —More than one-half of the average weekly viewing by these children occurs between 4:30 p.m. and 11:00 p.m.[8]
   —Television is the only medium children use day after day.[9]
   —Younger children prefer programs designed for children; but "by the time children leave elementary school, their preferences encompass most categories of programming watched by adults."[10]
   —Children view approximately three hours of television advertising each week, or about 50 advertisements per day.[11]
4. Viewing and learning:
   —Certain program techniques and formats "significantly influence attention and facilitate learning."[12]
   —Research has shown that there was greater learning when combined audio-visual techniques were used than "when [a] program was presented in only one modality (either auditory or visual)."[13]
   —Children learn a wide variety of facts, skills, concepts, and attitudes from Sesame Street and the Electric Company.[14]
   —Television develops values. "It has been shown that ratios of violence and the social characteristics of aggressors and victims can affect adult viewers' perceptions of society."[15]
5. Commercials and learning:
   —Children under eight have substantial difficulty comprehending the difference in purpose between commercials and programs.[16]
   —". . . children attend to and learn from commercials."[17] Commercials create positive attitudes toward and desire for products. Younger children are more susceptible to this effect. "Scepticism increases with age."[18]
   —Children learn nutritional information when it is included in commercials.[19]
   —"Exposure to medicine advertising does, to a certain extent, influence a child's conception of illness and medicine."[20]
   —A single commercial does affect children's short-term social beliefs regarding jobs appropriate for women.[21]

If television is here to stay, and if it consumes as many waking hours in the lives of young children as current statistics suggest, how can teachers, parents, and others maximize the positive influences of television? How can teachers use television or teach children how to view television in order to promote the most desirable social outcomes of this current technology? Planned classroom use of current programs, development of critical viewing in children, assistance to parents for mediating their children's viewing, and actions to influence the content of future programming are movements in this direction.

Planned Classroom Use

The early childhood teacher can use television to promote learning in numerous disciplines. In the first years of Head Start, media equipment was brought into the classrooms for the purpose of encouraging reading, language, and mathematics skills. Several specific programs have been designed to reach children in a given content area. Sesame Street was a breakthrough of educational television. The prime focus of this program has been on reading readiness and on the decoding process in reading. However, when Sesame Street was adopted for German television, 30 per cent of the content emphasized social studies.[22] Other recent programs have been directed toward specific social studies goals. One example is Vegetable Soup. Both Vegetable Soup and Sesame Street are used to teach social studies in early childhood classes.

Direct Social Studies Goals and Content. The scene is an early childhood classroom with a group of children seated comfortably on rugs and viewing a pre-selected segment on the school television service. The teacher's goal for this activity is to promote positive attitudes toward children with different cultural backgrounds. The enabling activities include the use of food—in this case, bread—to develop the concepts that:

1. The foods we eat represent our cultural heritages.
2. While bread and other carbohydrates differ from culture to culture, there are some noticeable similarities.
3. The basic need for and use of bread is the same in most cultures.

These concepts are to be developed by viewing three segments from an educational television program in conjunction with planned activities in the classroom.

The three television segments stress cultural diversity through the use of several program techniques. The first segment is presented in animation; the second views different breads in relation to the cultures of various people; and the third shows children making and eating Navaho Fry Bread. Each part of the program is timed for the attention span of young children, and they watch attentively. As the children watch the segment showing different kinds of bread, they identify with what they see on the screen and they respond in the following ways:

"Oh, there's *my* bread. We eat that at home."

"That's Italian bread . . . Oh, no! We eat *that* too."

"I can make that."

"Where are the biscuits? I didn't see any."

Following the viewing, children make their own choices for personal involvement in activities that the teacher has prepared to reinforce concepts already learned and to explore new, but related, materials. Classroom activities which enable the teacher and children to interact with each other and with physical materials include:

1. making bread
2. interviewing the school's dietitian for her recipe for bread
3. making a chart listing everyone's favorite bread
4. reproducing breads in art form, such as clay or a drawing
5. visiting the baker several blocks from the school

Baking bread proved to be the most exciting activity for the children, as well as for their teachers. As the children shared the experiences and consulted with children who were familiar with the recipe being made, they began to increase their knowledge about other cultures. Positive attitudes were being internalized, even though the children were unaware of the effect this activity had on their values, feelings, and attitudes. The verbal interaction during the process of making the bread provided insight into the children's thinking and helped the teachers to observe the processes the children used in restructuring their thoughts and ideas. The knowledge of contributions of other cultural groups and the personal involvement of the children with these contributions helped reduce fear and anxiety about people in other cultures. The television program stimulated the children's desire to know more about other people. It provided a tangible structure for building social values.

The overall goals of Vegetable Soup have been to assist young children in their understanding of ethnic groups from whom they are racially or geographically isolated.[23] They

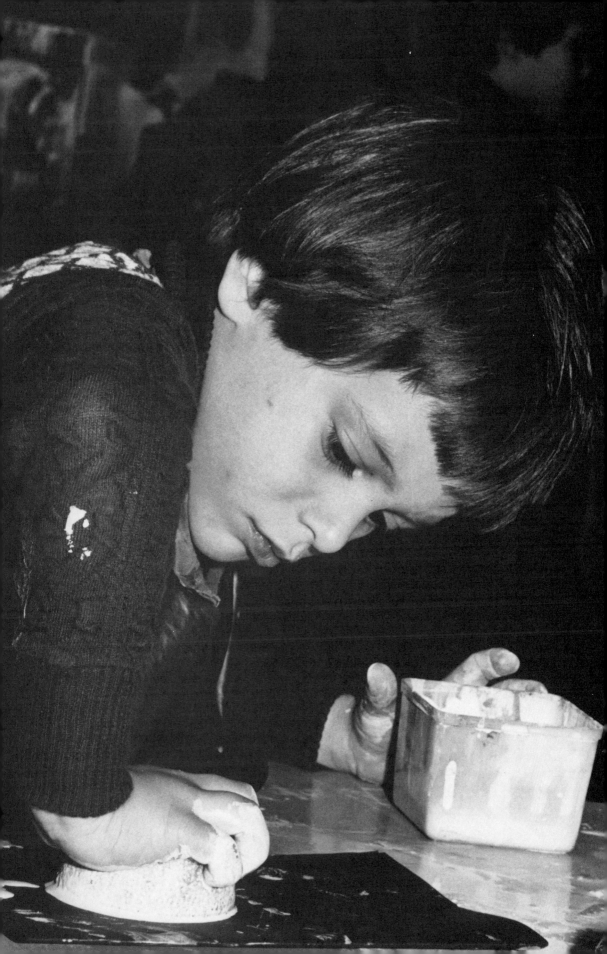

were planned to help mitigate the effects of racial isolation and/or prejudice. Other goals have been to help children appreciate different points of view and styles of living, to teach cooperation with different groups, and to develop respect for similarities and differences among individuals and among groups. Research data on these series suggest that the programs have a recognizable effect on promoting positive intergroup attitudes.[24]

Indirect Social Studies Goals and Content.[25] Ms. Gloria Cetron teaches kindergarten in the Sleepy Hollow Elementary School in Fairfax County, Virginia. Her class is an example of a multicultural community similar to that of many neighborhoods in America today. She has children from Pakistan, Guatemala, Iraq, and Vietnam, as well as children from various parts of the United States. Many children enter her classroom unable to speak or understand English. This may be their first social experience in a new country. She uses Sesame Street to accomplish goals in reading, mathematics, and social studies. Ms. Cetron believes planned viewing of television in the classroom does not need to be a passive experience. There are many occasions where children need to sit still, to listen, and to watch so that they can respond to a learning experience that has active emotional and intellectual involvement. The important elements of the learning experience are the quality of the social environment, the motivation of the child to become involved with the ideas and actions, and the relevance of the television program to the children's needs.

Ms. Cetron prepares the environment so the children have a warm, comfortable social experience during viewing time. Children sit close to one another. Shubnum from Pakistan puts her arm around Alliah from Iraq, and Kristi from Virginia places her seating rug nearby so she can sit close to them. Ms. Cetron encourages them to be comfortable and relaxed and to share actively the viewing experience together with her.

"What letter will we see today? Will it be a letter we already know?" Ms. Cetron says, in order to build suspense.

It is Mario's turn to operate the television, and he carries out his responsibilities with a certain dignity and seriousness. "Thank you, Mario," says Ms. Cetron, realizing that she is teaching courtesy and respect for others through her own actions.

The program appears. "It's the letter D!" Marsha exclaims.

"I can write D." "We already know D." "My name begins with D." "Look it's a dog." These are comments as the program begins.

"You are correct. We do know the letter D. You are my best students. Let's watch to learn what other words begin with the letter D." Ms. Cetron actively provides positive reinforcement, builds ego strength, and directs attention to the next scenes on the television.

The children in her class participate verbally in a skillful social interaction during the viewing while they are responding to the topic on the screen. They know it is all right to ask questions and they expect to learn. At the end of the planned viewing time, the television is turned off and the children talk together with their teacher. They talk about what they have just seen on the television. They relate it to knowledge from their own personal experiences. Because many of the children in this class have firsthand knowledge of other countries, other languages, and different traditions, the whole class benefits from this verbal exchange. Sometimes new materials on the television program provide a preparation for future class activities, and at other times information is a reinforcement of content already learned in the classroom. Ms. Cetron continuously mediates the content of the program and the special needs of the individual children in her classroom. She is consciously integrating social education and other academic areas with the assistance of television media.

Informed Use of Television

The use of television in the classroom for social studies goals involves four major steps: (1) preplanning, (2) previewing activities with the children, (3) viewing procedures, and (4) follow-up.

Preplanning. Preplanning includes all of the preparations the teacher makes outside of class. It includes the decision to use television. Below are several preplanning activities:

1. Plan the use of equipment before turning on the set. Television should not be used merely because it is available, a handy baby sitter, or an alternative teaching technique. There should be a good reason for using this medium.
2. Clearly state the teaching goals and select experiences to reach these goals.
3. Use program guides to determine a match between your goals and the producer's goals and objectives. To assist teachers in using media for instructional purposes, a variety of teacher's manuals and guides have been published. Boards of Education in regions across the country publish bulletins and guides for media and telecommunications. The Division of Educational Planning and Support (DEPS) is the center for library and media services for the Board of Education in New York City. The Board of Education in New York City publishes a yearly manual of instruction to accompany specific radio and television programs. Other cities and counties have similar publications to complement their programs. Subscriptions to radio and television guides help teachers direct students to programs with relevant information. Most guides provide details of the program and suggest complete lesson plans for each program presented. For example, the *Vegetable Soup Parent/Teacher Guide* states the broad topics used on programs and rec-

ommends ways to help students develop methods of inquiry and understanding of the world in which they live.[26] A *Teacher's Guide to the Humanities* for "Word and Image" and for "The Human Adventure" has a suggested lesson plan for each radio and television program.[27] It includes an introduction, statement of purpose, preparation guides, activities, and materials for extension and expansion of concepts.

4. Preview the program. Some school systems have a library of television programs which can be viewed through special television hook-ups. The advantages of previewing television programming are similar to those for previewing films. The teacher learns the length and content of the program prior to use and can determine the relevance of the materials to the teaching goals and to the current needs of the children. Also, many programs designed for other content areas can be adapted to meet current social studies needs. For example, while Sesame Street has a prime focus on language development, many aspects of the program can be used to promote goals in social studies.

5. Look for ways to stimulate questions, inquiries, and group discussion. What questions do you anticipate? What questions do children ask directly or indirectly?

Previewing Activities. Previewing activities are those experiences that prepare the children for the content of the program. If children know what to look for on the screen, they will be more alert and will gain more information. Planned activities prior to viewing are motivators for high interest. For example, the Vegetable Soup series included a multicultural program showing a variety of hair colors, textures, and fashionable hair styles. Before viewing this segment, one teacher brought hand mirrors to class so children could observe their own hair. He encouraged them to notice varieties, discuss likenesses and differences, and ask questions. The teacher took note of the questions his class asked and knew which ones would be answered during the program. He used the students' unanswered questions, general conversations, and actions to provide direction for follow-up activities.

Viewing procedures. Viewing procedures are important to the children's attention span. Room preparation is essential for optimum viewing. The screen should be large enough to accommodate all of the viewers, and children need to be seated in comfortable positions which enable easy viewing. Special attention may be necessary for children with visual or auditory problems.

Follow-up. Follow-up provides opportunity to move in the directions that relate to the individual children's needs. Children can expand upon the information given, interact with the ideas and concepts presented in a concrete fashion, have closure on some concepts, and begin to ask questions that will result in new inquiries and new problems to solve. Allow children to respond to the program in their own styles. If the segment has been of particular interest, children will immediately begin a dialogue about what they have seen. Assist the children to relate the program to their own experiences. For example, after viewing the segment on hair, help the children see the relationship between what they observed in their mirrors prior to the show with the information they saw on television. Since this program was concerned with promoting positive ethnic attitudes, the classroom teacher pointed out the relationship between this particular segment about hair and the concept of differences and similarities of ethnic groups. He helped the children expand the information to other related disciplines; he used knowledge from biology to explain that children inherit certain characteristics such as hair color and texture; and he utilized the information to dispel prejudicial attitudes or value judgments about kinds and colors of hair. All members of the class were able to appreciate one another and to strengthen their own self-concepts.

Follow-up activities vary with the content of the program and the needs of the children in the classroom. Some extensions of the viewing will be carried out by individual children with particular interests; others by small groups.

Developing Critical Viewing Skills

Research cited earlier in this chapter indicates that children are learning information, attitudes, and social values from the programs and from the commercials they view each day. Yet children engage in most of their television viewing outside of the classroom and beyond the direct leadership of the teacher and the formal educational institutions.

One goal of social education is the development of analytical and critical thinking skills for decision-making and problem-solving in society. Classroom teachers can consciously plan to help children develop these skills in relation to television viewing.

Today's young people have the opportunity to become aware of social issues through the media. They can become involved in, work through, and try to solve problems around current events. They may understand and view the world in a more global manner because television brings the world into their homes.

John and David were watching television in their Bethesda, Maryland, home when the program was interrupted to show the United States President's helicopter returning him to the White House from the Bethesda Naval Hospital. Their older sisters realized they could see the hospital from the school playground in back of their home. So all four children ran to the top of the hill.

"There's the President's helicopter. I see it in the sky," shouted David. He ran back down the hill, rushed into the house, and said, "There's the President's helicopter. I see it on TV. It *was* up in the sky." Then he rushed back up the hill to watch it disappear from view in real life. What an exciting piece of knowledge for these children! Television is a moving picture of real life. The news on television shows us events that are actually occurring in life. But are these events all happening while we watch them? Did some events occur before we watched them? Is everything on television factual?

Young children are not able to understand the difference in purpose between commercials and programs. Do they know the difference between news about war and movies about war? Can they tell the difference between situation comedies and real-life drama? As you talk about television programming with the children in your class, you may be able to recognize their misconceptions and misinterpretations. Then you can decide the next actions you should take to help the children in your class understand what they are viewing and to develop skills of comprehension, analysis, and judgment.

Ms. Johnson began a series of social studies lessons in the day-care center because children were talking about a program they had seen. The program was "Roots." Most of them had watched it on television. They had observed the drama and the pathos. Their parents were watching. Their friends were watching. It was an important event in their lives, and they could not stop talking about it. So Ms. Johnson joined with them in the conversation. She found out that they wanted to know more about Africa because some parents had said their ancestors had come from Africa. They had many questions. "Is Africa like Brooklyn? Is Africa as far away as South Carolina?" Ms. Johnson responded. "Yes, Africa is far away." (Yet it was as close as their living rooms.) Then Ms. Johnson began to ask questions about what the children had seen and what they would like to know. What did they notice from the program that they would like to share with the other children? Was Africa similar to or different from their block in Brooklyn? In what ways? Would they like to know the foods that grow in Africa today? How could the class find out more information?

As a result of these discussions and the high interest level of the children, Ms. Johnson went to the public library and began to research. She found pictures of foods grown in Africa and pictures of the plains, the forests, and the cities. She made a big map of Africa on which the children placed drawings of food grown in Africa. The children began to realize that Africa is a real place in the world—as real as Brooklyn. Children who identified with Africa felt good about themselves. They felt good about their parents, as they saw a supportive atmosphere between the day-care center and their homes. All children in the class felt good about the things they were learning. They also began to question values. How should people behave toward one another? How can people understand each other better? Throughout the week that "Roots" was being shown, and for several weeks afterward, the teacher used the children's viewing as a springboard for teaching history, geography, human relations, global issues, and values. Both Ms. Johnson and her class had a valuable learning experience as a result of discussing television viewed outside the classroom.

One way the classroom teacher can begin to relate television viewing with social education goals is to talk about the programs that the children are currently watching. What are children viewing? When do they watch television? Who watches with them: their parents, siblings, friends? What do they like best? What did they learn from watching television yesterday? Questions like these are open-ended. They encourage children to talk about their current television viewing and what it means to them. The information gained during these conversations will help the teacher to assess the children's viewing patterns and their conceptions of what they are viewing. The teacher will be able to translate the children's needs into future social education activities and learning sequences.

Several topics with social significance are:

1. Fantasy and reality. Is the story on television fictional or factual? Carolyn is eleven and she believes that the situation comedies are a real portrayal of life. How does this shape the view that Caroline has about herself and about what her life ought to be as she grows up? How does it influence her daily behavior?

2. Consumerism. Children view many commercials. How does this affect their desires for products? How does it influence their interactions with their parents? Will they feel diminished if they do not or cannot own the latest item advertised on television?

3. Parent/child relations. In what ways does television viewing affect family relationships?

4. Value judgments. What do children learn about violence and aggression, about personal relationships, about global relationships, about what one should laugh at or consider humorous from watching television?

5. Options for recreation. Are there other ways to enjoy free time? Is it fun to read a book, paint a picture, talk with a friend? How many activities do you, or can you, enjoy? Should television be your only source of relaxation?

The above topics are a starting point. Classroom teachers will add to this list as they explore the use of television with the children in their classes.

Assisting Parents

Today's parents are especially concerned with their children's education. Many parents are expressing their concerns by the way they vote at the polls, through active leadership in Parent/Teacher Associations and other organizations, and with planned involvement in the education of their children outside the school system. Among their concerns are the uses and the effects of television. This concern is expressed by parents at all economic levels and across cultural groups.

The social room was filling with parents who had set aside this morning to come to the elementary school and with teachers who had been given release time. They were talking in small groups over coffee until the meeting began. Then the Director for the Community-Based Parent/Early Childhood Center, who had planned this meeting, encouraged all of them to bring their coffee and sit together.[28] The meeting began. The purpose of this meeting was to bring together three important groups (parents, teachers, and those involved in community services) to talk about questions, problems, and needs of parents and children in the community. Did parents have any problems they would like to talk about? Was there anything special they needed for their family? The warmth and openness of the Director was infectious, and soon parents were beginning to express themselves. This morning the topic turned to television. Parents were worried about the amount of time their children view television while parents are at work, whether or not the programs are good for their children, how many snacks their children eat as they watch television, and how to encourage their children to participate in other activities. They questioned their own use of television as a baby sitter, as a means to keep children off the street, or as an inexpensive family activity in which the programs that appeal to their older children are not appropriate for the younger children. What should they do about these problems? What could they do?

As the group expressed its concerns, the leader skillfully asked them questions that encouraged them to think about their personal involvements and to respond with their own solutions. "What do you think you would do in this situation? What would you like to do? Has anyone else had a similar problem? What has worked for you?" Together the members of this group of parents and teachers talked about their experiences. They shared information, suggestions, and ideas. In this informal setting, everyone felt comfortable. People with difficult problems received sympathy and support from other members of the group. Most parents felt less isolated when they talked with other parents who had similar experiences.

The Director suggested that parents try to join their children in some television viewing, making it a shared experience.[29] Then they can talk about the programs they are watching together and about the programs that the children have watched without them. During these conversations they may learn what their children think about and how they feel. This will give them opportunities to share ideas, express values, clarify misunderstandings, and build closer family relationships.

Everyone had a sense of accomplishment. The members of the group decided to try out some of the suggestions they had learned. Then they would meet again next month to discuss their progress.

Classroom teachers can find many ways to share ideas with parents. Teachers and parents can build together on their strengths to help each other promote positive social learnings from television viewing. Teachers may want to initiate a meeting similar to the one described above. They may share in a planned study group through the P.T.A.; or they may speak with parents on an informal basis, invite them to the classroom, or interest them through the work of their children. As teachers and parents communicate with each other in formal or informal settings, they will share information and ideas that will be a learning experience for all concerned groups.

Other Media

Media devices other than television continue to be used in early childhood classrooms to offer diversity in teaching methods and materials and to enhance the ongoing social education curriculum. Though the list of available equipment varies from school to school, it usually includes opaque projectors, overhead projectors, filmstrips, movies, phonographs, and tape recorders. Some teachers may have access to cameras and audiovisual tape cassette equipment. Classroom teachers have had experience with most of these teaching tools. The following paragraphs emphasize use of equipment in situations where children are actively involved.

Overhead projectors allow the teacher to face the students and to speak to them while writing or drawing material that is clearly visible to a large group of children. With young children it can provide a spontaneity in storytelling similar to the flannel graph. Children can display their own creative work or research information to their classmates on the overhead projector. This active technique requires teacher supervision, but it goes beyond the "show and tell" periods by giving the child the opportunity to prepare the materials and gain facility with technical equipment. It adds a new dimension by enlarging the child's work.

Phonographs are used for creative dramatics, stories, singing, and music to accompany work, play, or rest periods. Sturdy phonographs give children an opportunity to operate the equipment by themselves. They can select and listen to records of their own choices within the limits of the situation. They learn to share together, to spend quiet times alone, and to accept responsibility for material property within their own living spaces.

Photography provides numerous opportunities for social education. Children can record their world in pictures. Changes in the neighborhood, field trips, children baking bread or investigating their world, and the physical growth of children throughout the year can all be recorded with a camera by the children or by the teacher. Pictures taken of children or of their projects provide an excellent opportunity to develop the scientific method. Later the information recorded on film can be described in written words. This encourages reading skills, too. Photos accompanied by stories of children in the classroom build ego-strength and a feeling of belonging.

Tape recorders afford many opportunities to learn about the physical world and to interact socially. Children increase their skills involving speech and sound, collecting oral data, recording class reports, and recording and analyzing information. Children can take portable sets into the community to record data about individuals and activities of social significance. For example, a child can record a great-grandmother's story about "when I was a child." This tape can be brought back to class for all the children to hear. Children at EveryChild Day Care Center (Chapter Two) could have used a tape recorder as they went into the community to try to solve the problem of litter. Small children are capable of using this equipment under the guidance of a more mature person.

Audio-visual tapes and movie cameras are sometimes available to teachers. These technologies more nearly approximate the types of media young children will be using every day as they grow older. Already teenagers are making their own films in many high school classes. These technologies are personal extensions of movies and of television. Now some tapes can be played on television sets. The classroom use of this equipment is similar to having the children make their own television programs, in which they are the writers of the script, the directors, and the actors. Classroom teachers will enjoy experimenting with this equipment.

Future uses of technology include advances in the use of media. Projections for picture telephones, interactive television, and other extensions of audio-visual equipment are likely.

Children can become active learners in the use of all of the above technologies. They may control the use of the media and interact with the physical environment as well as the social environment. The use of media provides a format for the development of social studies concepts and an opportunity to become skillful in social science processes.

Summary

Technological advances in our society have contributed to our children's orientation toward media. In view of continued improvements in technology, we can expect an increase in the use of a wide variety of audio-visual equipment and in television. The phenomenon has had and continues to exhibit profound effects on the behavior patterns of our children. It affects the way we learn social behaviors. Teachers, parents, and other interested adults are seeking effective uses of television and other media to promote the positive aspects of social education through media.

Footnotes

[1] George Gerbner, *Television Violence Profile*, National Institute of Mental Health (Washington, D.C.: U.S. Government Printing Office, 1974-1975).

[2] Richard P. Adler, *Research on the Effects of Television Advertising on Children: A Review of the Literature and Recommendations for Future Research.* (Washington, D.C.: U.S. Government Printing Office, NSF Grant No. APR 75-10126, 19).

[3] A. C. Nielsen Co, *The Television Audience* (Chicago: A. C. Neilsen Company, 1976).

[4] Wilbur Schramm, J. Lyle, and E. B. Parker, *Television in the Lives of Our Children* (Stanford, Calif.: Stanford University Press, 1961).

[5] Nielson, 1976.

[6] Adler, *Research on the Effects of Television Advertising on Children*, p. 12.

[7] A. C. Nielsen, *The Television Audience*, 1975.

[8] *Ibid.*

[9] Adler, *Research on the Effects of Television Advertising on Children.*

[10] *Ibid.*, p. 18.

[11] *Ibid.*, p. 20.

[12] Gerald Lesser, *Children and Television; Lessons from Sesame Street* (New York: Random House, 1974); Edward Palmer, "Formative Research in Educational Television Production: The Experience of the Children's Television Workshop," in W. Schramm (Ed.), *Quality in Instructional Television* (Hawaii: University Press of Hawaii, 1972).

[13] Wilber Schramm, "What the Research Says," in W. Schramm (Ed.), *Quality in Instructional Television.*

[14] Barbara R. Fowles, Statement presented at Hearings before the Subcommittee on Communications of the Committee on Interstate and Foreign Commerce, House of Representatives (Washington, D.C.: U.S. Government Printing Office, Serial No. 94-53, 1975).

[15] George Gerbner and Larry P. Gross, "Violence Profile No. 7: Trends in Network Television and Viewer Conceptions of Social Reality: 1967-1974," un-published manuscript (The Annenberg School of Communications, University of Pennsylvania, 1975).

[16] Adler, p. vii.

[17] *Ibid.*, p. v.

[18] *Ibid.*, p. 96; Thomas S. Robertson and John R. Rossiter, "Children and Commercial Persuasion: An Attribution Theory Analysis," *Journal of Consumer Research* 1:6 (1974): 13-20; Scott Ward, "Effects of Television Advertising on Children and Adolescents," Research supported by National Institute for Mental Health and by the Marketing Science Institute, June 1971.

[19] Adler, p. ix.

[20] *Ibid.*, p. 96.

[21] *Ibid.*, p. 54.

[22] Lisa Kuhmerker, "When Sesame Street Becomes Sesamestrasse: Social Education for Preschoolers Comes to Television," *Social Education* 40:1 (January 1976): 34-37.

[23] *Vegetable Soup: Bread Segment*, Bureau of Mass Communication (Albany, New York: New York State Education Department, 1975).

[24] Luberta Mays and E. Henderson and S. Seidman, *On Meeting Real People: An Evaluation Report on "Vegetable Soup,"* (New York: Medgar Evers College and The Research Foundation of the City University of New York, 1975).

[25] Personal interview with Ms. Gloria Cetron, Fairfax, Virginia, August 1978.

[26] *Parent/Teacher Guide: Vegetable Soup*, Bureau of Mass Communication (Albany, New York: New York State Education Department, 1975).

[27] *Teacher's Guide to the Humanities*, (New York: Board of Education of the City of New York, 1969).

[28] Community-Based Parent/Early Childhood Center is a community project at Medgar Evers College of the City University of New York.

[29] J. Singer and J. L. Singer, *Partners in Play: Parents, Teachers and Children*, (New York: Harper and Row, 1976).

6
Children Learning and Using Social Studies Content

Alicia L. Pagano

The previous chapters of this bulletin describe children growing, making decisions, solving problems, and becoming citizens within the setting of the school. The importance of parents in the social development of children is emphasized. Recognition is given to a growing concern for the influence of media on the development of social learning and moral decision-making.

Each of these specific topics concerning young children is presented with a point of view that integrates social studies curriculum and a developmental, interactionist theory of learning. This final chapter focuses directly on the content and methodology of the social studies as a basis for organizing teaching in early childhood education. It gives the classroom teacher a concrete definition of social studies in early childhood, and it provides examples of learning experiences based on the knowledge from the social science disciplines.

Introduction

Early childhood teachers are especially cognizant of the social needs of the developing child and of the importance of social education for young children. Social education has traditionally been a prime goal of preschool programs. In the past, many nursery schools have considered "socialization" the main function of the program and have emphasized "getting along with other children" or "preparing children to share with others."[1] Social learning is an important goal of education at all levels, but when it is stated in the general terminology of "socialization," it seems too vague to help today's classroom teacher to plan and assess social learning. Most teachers are seeking greater precision in describing the content and sources for social education in the classroom.

Currently, social educators are taking a critical look at relevant curriculum and are attempting to relate the needs of young children to social studies content. Research indicates the importance of building a strong, basic foundation for social education in preschool programs and in the early years of elementary schools.[2] Thus, when children enter the upper grades they will have acquired the appropriate social studies skills and will have the motivation and interest for continued inquiry and learning in this area.[3] Social studies should be included in early childhood curriculum guides along with other academic areas, such as pre-reading, pre-mathematics, art, and music.[4] Also, concern for support of social studies in the early years has been shown at state levels of education. For example, recommendations to the New York State Education Department for future curricula say, "the state should mandate social studies K-12" and "a minimum of 30 minutes daily, or its equivalent over the week, be spent on the instruction of social studies."[5]

In order to build strong social studies foundations during the early years, it is important to have specific, planned social studies goals in early childhood, with stated social studies content, activities, and evaluation techniques.[6] To accomplish these goals, it is necessary to begin with a clear definition of social studies in early childhood. One possible way to do this is to approach the social studies through the social science disciplines. This chapter suggests that the content of social studies in early childhood finds its base in current knowledge in the social sciences.

The approach to early childhood education is not one of a passive accumulation of facts. Rather, it is planning social environments in which the contents of the social sciences are "brought into relation with the structures and functions that are spontaneously active in the child's mind."[7] Methods for organizing teaching based on social sciences and upon child psychology will be examined.

Subject Matter and Learning

Social education in the early years finds its basis in the development of the child within society and in the subject matter and methodology of the social studies.

Most psychologists agree that the early years of a child's life are those in which the foundations for future behaviors and attitudes are established. Piaget's theory of cognitive development suggests that new cognitive structures in children are based upon existing structures within the child.[8] When children receive new information, it is processed through the knowledge the child already possesses. The child who has had rich cognitive experiences in the world has an advantage in decision-making and in processing new information. Varied, planned experiences in social studies increase a child's ability to process information helpful for social growth.

The findings and theories of cognitive psychologists are being applied more extensively to the social studies curriculum. Through the intellectual foundations of the social studies, children become involved with the current available thinking in today's world. Teaching based on the knowledge of the social sciences provides young children with information and skills that improve their de-

cision-making, enhance their problem-solving, and develop competent, self-directed citizens.

One of the assumptions of the Taba social studies curriculum for kindergarten through sixth grade is that the "intake of information and the cognitive organization of information are major ways in which the key processes of assimilation and accommodation [from Piaget] appear."[9] According to Bruce Joyce, "the content and procedures involved in the social studies can prepare a child to participate effectively in his [or her] society."[10] Bernard Spodek points out that the ability to deal with one's surroundings "requires that an individual have access to certain information about the world."[11] Also the individual needs skills in processing worldly information to organize it so that generalizations can be made and new information can be integrated into a developing knowledge system.

Following these thoughts, it can be seen that the content of the social studies curriculum can be taught from the child's vantage point.[12] Planned learning activities stemming from the child's own experiences and perceived needs provide opportunities for new growth. The subject matter of the social studies curriculum offers new facts, information, and ideas for this expansion and growth. Both Dewey and Piaget describe this process in a similar manner. Dewey states that "experiences in order to be educative must lead out into an expanding world of subject matter, a subject matter of facts of information or ideas. This condition is satisfied only as the educator views teaching and learning as a continuous process of reconstruction of experience."[13]

Content

Educators of young children who are taking a specific interest in the area of social studies seek to clarify a framework for social education in early childhood. They look for ways to build strong foundations for positive self-images, good citizenship, and the ability to function effectively in a world in which there is increasing individual autonomy at the same time as there is an increasing interdependency among individuals and nations.[14] Foundations for individual growth and social improvement must be built early in life as the basis for the goals of an effective social studies program in early education.

These goals are in line with the general goal of social studies education in all classroom levels. Despite the continual controversy over the definition and content of the field of social studies, most social studies educators agree that citizenship education is the prime goal of the social studies.[15] In addition, some educators suggest that social studies should be defined by its instructional goal, rather than by the content. Barr, who takes this view, says it avoids the problem of conflicts about what is to be included or excluded from the content of the social studies curriculum. He defines citizenship as the goal of social studies and then describes the content and methodology according to three traditions which have their sources in basic philosophical views of the world. These three approaches are:

1. Social studies taught as citizenship transmission, in which teachers "transmit to the young a conception both of an ideal society and of ideal citizenship."
2. Social studies taught as a social science, in which "young people shall acquire the knowledge, skills, and devices of particular social science disciplines to the end that they become effective as citizens."
3. Social studies taught as reflective inquiry, in which "students learn the process of decision-making in a sociopolitical context."[16]

Citizenship education is a very broad goal for one subject area. It could be viewed as the goal of all education. The NEA Committee on Social Studies in 1916, while seeking to place social studies goals within the context of the overall goals of American education, defined the "conscious and constant" purposes of the American schools to be the "cultivation of good citizenship."[17]

Taken in this broad sense, such a goal includes mathematics and the ability to compute time, distance, and personal finances. It includes reading and writing because these skills are essential to effective functioning in today's society. Following this line of thought, *all* learning could be considered social studies and *all* teaching in early childhood could be called social education. At one level of thinking, this is true. All knowledge is one; but this totality can be divided into smaller, discrete categories or subsystems for purposes of organized, in-depth study.

Today's vast amount of knowledge calls for a specialization in areas of study, as well as for generalized study. *Specialization* requires concentrated research and the study of narrow areas of thought. It requires looking at a circumscribed body of knowledge with great depth and precision. *Generalization* requires a broad overview that often combines interdisciplinary and multidisciplinary knowledge. This can be illustrated by the scientist who researches the structure of the walls of individual human cells and by the general physician who observes a person's overall health. Both of these professionals provide a necessary health-care service.

Because traditional bodies of knowledge can be studied in specialized forms and because they can be combined to form new areas of study, it becomes more difficult to separate educational content into discrete subject areas. Disciplines are being combined in so many new ways that it is impossible to be knowledgeable in each of them. Psycholinguistics, bio-geography, and socio-economics are examples of interdisciplinary studies. Each of these areas combines elements of two or more separate fields to form a meaningful new area. These interdisciplinary approaches remind us that although all knowledge is one, there are reasons for making arbitrary distinctions between disciplines.

The concepts of specialization and generalization are apparent in early childhood education. Teachers are generalists when they approach teaching and learning from an interdisciplinary point of view; they are specialists when they concentrate on precise information from specific disciplines.

The content of the social sciences used in conjunction with content from other disciplines provides the totality of information available for optimum citizenship education. The social sciences as separate areas of study and in combination with other disciplines provide the organizing basis for the content of the social studies.

According to the constitution of the National Council for the Social Studies, the term *social studies* "is used to include: the social science disciplines and those areas of inquiry which relate to the role of the individual in a democratic society designed to protect his or her integrity and dignity and which are concerned with the understanding and solution of problems dealing with social issues and human relations."[18]

Social studies is that area of the curriculum that focuses on the study of human beings. Ellis writes that "although the language arts, mathematics, and natural sciences certainly deal with human experience in the form of ideas, skills, and products, it is the special function of social studies to have people as its subject matter . . . . Social studies is learning about people and the various ways in which they interact with each other and with the various environments in which they find themselves."[19] He goes on to say, "Social studies is about the students themselves—their present needs, their possible futures, their sharing and growing awareness of themselves and others around them."[20]

In early childhood education, the content areas of social studies can all be defined in terms of the personal view of the young child because young children will generally interact by relating information and actions to themselves in their present situation. Social studies provides an excellent opportunity to study one's self and to arrive at a meaningful understanding of one's self in relation to society and to the world in which we live.

Below are definitions of the major disciplines of the social sciences presented in personal terms. These definitions do not include the newer subdisciplines that have emerged, nor do they include interdisciplinary approaches. However, if the major disciplines are described in terms helpful to educators working with young children, the same methodology can be used to place other areas of knowledge into the same format. These definitions are:

History—my past
Geography—the environment in which I live
Psychology—my needs and desires
Sociology—how I fit into the society in which I live
Anthropology—how my culture has shaped my life
Political Science—the influence I exert upon others and the influence they exert upon me
Economics—how I am supported financially[21]

Many early childhood educators focus on an interdisciplinary or generalist's approach to content. They prefer not to divide the day's activities into separate learnings in "reading," "mathematics," "social studies," etc. However, as was discussed earlier in this chapter, it is important at times to specialize and to make subdivision in the areas of knowledge. In early childhood, as in the upper grades, social studies content, activities, and skills have their basis in these arbitrarily subdivided disciplines of the social sciences. Young children are able to understand social studies as described above if the materials and the experiences are based upon their own personal backgrounds and are presented at their developmental level.

Young children live in the present, the "here and now," They gradually develop the concepts of abstract thinking and of space and time relations. In fact, the main keys to the child's mental growth, according to Piaget, are:

1. The importance of the child's own action upon the world. Children learn from acting upon their environment and from interacting with others in a social context.

2. The way these actions are "a process of inward building-up; that is, of forming within the child's mind a continually extending structure corresponding to the world outside."[22]

The personal definitions of the social sciences support the view that teachers of young children should "provide a present which is relevant to the future, but which is at the same time consistent with the developing abilities of young children."[23] As children begin to interact with others and to act upon their environment, the content of the social studies provides an essential body of knowledge from which they can draw. This does not mean that the teacher is pouring factual information into the child, or that the child is subjected to rote learning of historical data. Rather, the content of the social sciences becomes a source of information, and the methodology of the social sciences becomes a tool of process from which the children can begin to structure their own worlds. The teacher, knowing and recognizing this body of knowledge, can prepare optimum learning environments, ask the sequential questions, and suggest activities that will enable the children to interact in this environment toward the goals of citizenship. (Observe the questions that Ms. Banks asked the kindergarteners as they read the story related in Chapter Two.) The quality and the quantity of knowledge available to children as they build upon previous structures to organize new ones will determine the cumulative level of learning.

This background of previous knowledge is important in all areas of learning. One of the components for the development of creativity is a firm knowledge-base.[24] Children are not expected to read without the use of the tools of reading. Whether a teacher uses a phonics or a whole-word approach, reading as we know it would not be possible without the use of some symbolic code. It is a truism that young children need the tools of the social sciences in order to develop the concepts and skills for decoding the world in which they live.

As children learn to make decisions, they do so within the framework of their existing knowledge of the world. While they try to solve problems meaningful to them, they are searching for ways to understand themselves and to relate to the world around them. Teachers will turn to the social sciences to design activities based upon a perceived problem of the children. The social sciences provide resources in methodology and in content for efficient and effective means to solve these problems. The children will not be aware of the structures of the disciplines. We would not expect them to exclaim precociously, "Aha, I will use political science theories to help me solve this problem about litter in the street,' " But the teacher will use this knowledge to provide direction for the children. The teacher will call upon knowledge from psychology to select supportive activities to strengthen a child's weak ego. Information from sociology will be helpful in problems of leadership and classroom management.

Method

The method of the developmental interactionists in teaching young children is based upon recognition of qualitative differences in stages of cognitive development. It is also built upon a belief in the ability of children to learn through interacting with their environment.

Weybright in Chapter One of this book discusses the cognitive development of children and examines the differences in abilities of children based upon maturation and experience in the social world. The *developmental* view suggests that children's intellectual development is sequential, orderly, and irreversible.

The *interactive* approach identifies the way children learn in relation to their environment. Learning can be viewed from three particular theoretical approaches. In these views, the learner is either:

1. passive
2. active
3. interactive[25]

If children are viewed as passive, the behavior of the child is expected to be largely a product of environmental influences. The child is dependent upon knowledge which comes from the outside world and he or she has little input into this prepared environment. The child is acted upon by the outside world, and it is the responsibility of the teacher to provide the proper information to be absorbed by the child. If children are viewed as active, their underlying characteristics are inborn. It is nature, rather than nurture, that is important. The learning environment is merely a location for their natural unfolding. If children are viewed as interactive, they can be expected to give input into the environment and to be influenced by the environment. The interaction is a two-way relationship. Teaching becomes person-environment centered. The child brings something special to the learning environment, and the environment itself will determine directions for learning. In this view, the teacher and child learn together.

If children learn through acting upon their environment and interacting with people, the early childhood classroom should be a place where this type of behavior can readily occur. The classroom environment, since it is planned to facilitate learning, will recognize the needs of the children and will use methods congruent to these needs. The interactionist teacher will use methods that conform to the development of the child. A social studies curriculum that is based upon the development of the child will emphasize the actions of the children, rather than the overt leadership of the teacher. The teacher, who is responsible for the learning process and maintains the ultimate role of the leader, will prepare and sustain an environment in which young children can grow.

The interactionist's approach provides a rationale for a method of learning in a democratic society. As was shown by Nancy Wyner in Chapter Three, children prepare to become responsible citizens in a democracy through learning these skills in their early years.

The environment for learning indicates the educator's view of children and how they learn. One learning environment conducive to the interactive teaching style is the open classroom. Open areas give the learner the space to explore, the room to experiment, and the openness to make applications of personal discoveries. Early childhood learning areas often give the appearance of being more open than classes in elementary school settings because most preschool programs have learning centers.[26] However, learning centers in themselves do not require the use of an interactive approach. If children are continuously directed to specific centers in the classroom for definite periods of time, the children will be unable to act spontaneously upon their environment.

Role of the Teacher

The role of the teacher in the social education of young children involves two major concerns—content and methodology. The teacher's expertise in social education should be based on a firm grounding in the content of the social science disciplines, as well as on a knowledge of how the child learns. The child relates to the content through personal experience. Because it is in the active integration of experience that social studies is learned, the teacher has the opportunity to make the connections between the child's previous experiences and the content. New experiences need to be provided in the *old* framework to give them a context.

While some persons might argue that early childhood teachers do not need to know the content and methodology of the social sciences, we suggest that this is a naive view. It underestimates the capabilities of young children. Dewey urged that "mastery of subject matter and techniques of pedagogy should be internalized by all teachers."[27] Barr recently reinforced Dewey's statement by writing that "out of the knowledge selected and organized by informed teachers will come, it is hoped, a more enlightened understanding of the world as it is and a better quality of citizenship."[28]

It is the responsibility of the teacher to "select specific content to support and guide students."[29] Even at the early childhood age, children can learn knowledge that is expected for a person to function effectively in society. John Jarolimek says, "there is a body of information content that is necessary for ordinary civic and social literarcy."[30] Although Jarolimek was speaking about an expectation for knowledge in elementary-school children, the same is true at the preschool level.

Some educators might argue that Jerome Bruner was incorrect in saying children can learn any idea if it is taught with an intellectually honest method.[31] We affirm that social education in early childhood sets the foundation for future social behaviors. Children are continuously building new cognitive structures based on information they process through action and interaction in the environment. Shallow classroom experiences, void of content, are unlikely to produce effective, knowledgeable citizens; they are more apt to result in restless, bored, and inattentive students with antisocial behaviors. On the other hand, rich experiences grounded in the content and skills of the

social sciences provide a deep and broad background for future learning. They motivate children, give them confidence, and provide them with the ability to learn and behave independently within the society.

Traditionally, the early childhood teacher was more a guide than an instructor. The teacher taught rules for use of materials and for social living directly. This was especially true during the era when children were sent to nursery schools to gain skills in social development. Recent research in early childhood education supports the view of the teacher as an *active facilitator* of learning.[31] The teacher stimulates, questions, clarifies, supports, provides feedback, guides, diagnoses, and assists children in the process of reflective inquiry.[32] If the teacher does not possess a broad knowledge base, then inquiry may become depersonalized and turn into a mere memorization of readily available facts. The data for the solution to the problem may become detached from the life of the student and the information becomes "lessons to be learned."

The early childhood teacher is a democratic group leader who leads students in the study of significant problems. In the social studies curriculum, we find the foundations for many of the significant problems that interest young children. As Weybright and Wolf discussed in Chapters One and Two, the content of geography is used in making decisions about building the map of the neighborhood. The teacher who recognizes the basics of map-making will ask questions to stimulate the children and encourage them to think about what they are doing. This will lead to greater learning. Mays and Pagano, in Chapter Five, demonstrated the content of anthropology in action during the television segments depicting the ways different cultures make bread. The teacher who is knowledgeable in the social sciences will find it easier to use this as a spin-off to discuss other ways that culture shapes children's lives. A teacher with an understanding of the behavior of people in small groups or one who has used techniques of sociograms based on psychology and sociology will be much more efficient in organizing the learning environment. A teacher with managerial skills will recognize and employ leadership strategies to promote a democratic class environment. In each of the above examples, children are using social science content and methodology. In this context, the social sciences are recognized as the prime source for social education in early childhood.

Using Social Studies in the Classroom

The goal of Together We Stand Day-Care Center is to promote positive feelings about self and to encourage sharing and working together in the community. Three learning activities from this center provide examples for the use of social studies content in specific environmental settings.[33] Most of the activities emphasize the active involvement of children through inquiry, interaction, and personal discovery. They are not intended to pressure children for academic levels in public school. The activities do not divide the curriculum into separate subject areas of so many prescribed minutes for each day. They are planned to provide direction for expansion of ideas and content, for development of additional skills, and for enhancement of complex and interdependent, interpersonal relationships. The procedures employ three levels of teaching processes for working with young children. They are: messing around; extension of activities or ideas; and integration or tying together.[34] In each activity, the primary content area will be stated. Suggestions will be given for ways to expand, extend, and integrate the learning.

History

History, with a personal view, means the investigation of a child's own past. One activity that provides an environment for learning about a child's history is the building of a family tree. Making a family tree is a vehicle for the investigation. The messing around stage began with an open discussion with the four-year-olds about families. Following this activity, each child was given a cutout of a tree on which to place members of the family as perceived by the child. Family members were drawn by the child (but photos from home could have been used). Craig included his dog on his family tree.

A variety of extensions evolves from this activity. It promotes discussions of families, family sizes, family relationships, where families live, what families do together, ages of family members, and comparisons with families in other parts of the world. The child becomes aware of a personal history through questions and interaction. Children realize that they were babies in the past, that now they are growing, and that in the future they will be adults and will grow older. The concept of a life span begins to evolve. Ego strength is developed as the child feels acceptance in a family and in non-family groups. Other extensions include interviews with grandparents or senior citizens in the community who talk about "what it was like when I was a child." A child's family tree was displayed in the center on the child's birthday. With special recognition on that day, the family tree was expanded to include the special relationship of friends. The display indicated non-family and close friends. The children looked forward to their special days and to the discussion of their own lives and families.

This is an example of an activity that has its basis in the discipline of history and that is planned to meet the developmental needs of children who are living in the present and who are interested in personal information. The process may lead the class into inquiries related to sociology or anthropology. The concepts are integrated into the child's personal history and into the broader knowledge of history and research methodology. Foundations for positive attitudes toward history are beginning in this classroom.

Psychology

The development of a positive self-image and a strong ego are important psychological needs of children. Acceptance and understanding of self is the basis for beginning to accept others and to relate with others. There are many ways teachers can encourage children to feel good about themselves and to accept their individuality. Some of these are in the "hidden curriculum" and are manifested in the way the teacher talks with the children and shows respect for them as individuals. Even the arrangement of the classroom indicates the feelings for the children.

But the overt, planned curriculum can also provide an environment in which children learn that they are accepted and that they are important. One activity is *body-image drawing*. This activity is well-known to many early childhood teachers. It is presented here to focus on its use as a facilitator of concepts in psychology and to indicate new extensions of familiar activities. This activity can be carried out in several ways. Children lie on large, plain paper on the floor and another child or the teacher traces the outline of each child. The image is cut out and the child completes the picture by coloring, painting, or pasting cloth and other materials onto the form. Some children at the center are traced as if they were standing tall; others prefer to be traced in running or jumping movements. Upon completion, these body-images are hung on the walls. They are continuing items for initiating conversations about and with individual children. This activity can be expanded in many ways, depending upon the skills of the teacher and the interests of the children. The children's names can be written below the picture, and a short statement by each child can be written on a card below the cutout. These activities encourage social skills and provide motivation to enjoy and appreciate written communication and stimulate children to read, a skill so essential to social studies in later years.

One classroom used the body-image of a member to make a life-size puzzle. The puzzle was dissected so that children could name the parts of the body as they assembled the puzzle. The class selected Marva as the model for the puzzle and named it after her. Everyone was exuberant over this supersize game.

The content for these activities was derived from the field of psychology. Discussions and interactions growing out of these activities will integrate and reinforce positive images in children.

Geography

Map-making and map-reading are important skills in geography. *Mapping our room* is an excellent activity to develop spatial concepts. One group of children began mapping its room and finalized the project by building a three-dimensional model of it. This activity grew out of a discussion about the rearrangement of the room next door after it had been newly painted. The children began by talking about their room, observing its contents, and locating specific items in it. The teacher encouraged them and facilitated their learning at each level with questions and guidance. They measured the distances from wall to wall by walking and counting their steps. They noticed the spaces between the interest areas, and the lack of space when their cots were placed in the room during rest periods. Then they wanted to make a model in a cardboard box. As the class converted its observations and generalized measurements into the actual model, there were many interesting discussions about where a particular chair should be placed or on which side of the room a picture should be hung. In response to disagreements, children made new observations, shared ideas, and drew their own conclusions. Some of them made cutouts of the objects in the room and of the class members. They wanted a realistic model. Shashana made a drawing of the door. When the teacher questioned her about its size (it was much too small for entry), she made it again. The new door was exactly the same size as the previous one. She insisted that this size was perfect. The teacher recognized Shashana's level of spatial development and moved to the next activity. This model became a center of attraction for several weeks. It prompted discussions about comparisons in sizes (big chairs and little chairs, large windows and small windows), locations (near to or far away from), and possible rearrangements of the room.

This elementary project was a step toward developing the more advanced skills needed for map-making and map-reading. It was three-dimensional because the children were working at their current cognitive development levels. The content was geography, and the skills for this discipline were being taught with an intellectually honest method.

Summary

Social studies is a fundamental and essential subject areas for teaching and learning in early childhood. It can be planned around the structure and content of the social science disciplines. Through intentional lessons in social studies, the basic concepts, skills, and attitudes for relating to self, others, and the environment can be learned by young children. These experiences form a basic foundation for social education in later academic years. Given stimulating and appropriate social studies content and activities, children will be motivated through their own interest and involvement. They will be prepared to appreciate social studies education in the upper grades and in high school because they will have built positive attitudes toward the subject area.

The key element in a quality social studies program in early childhood education is the knowledge that the teacher brings to the classroom. Teachers of young children who have concrete backgrounds in the social sciences and in child development can use this knowledge to provide challenging cognitive environments in which children will participate actively. Teachers must take the initiative to expand the social science content of the curriculum with appropriate methodology. The teacher assures that the children integrate the learning experiences into their personal daily living through interactions and involvement.

Footnotes

[1] Richard E. Gross, "The Status of the Social Studies in the Public Schools of the United States: Facts and Impressions of a National Survey," *Social Education* 41:3 (March 1977): 194-200; Alicia L. Pagano, "Social Studies in Day Care" (Paper delivered at the Fifty-fifth Annual Meeting of the National Council for the Social Studies, Atlanta, Georgia, November 25, 1975).

[2] Raymond English, "Ten 'Discoveries' About Basic Learning," *Social Education* 41:2 (February 1977): 105-107.

[3] Lawrence Senesh, "The Economic World of the Child," *Instructor* 73 (March 1963): 7-8.

[4] Pagano, "Social Studies in Day Care."

[5] "Curriculum Mandate Revision," *Social Science Record* 14:2 (Winter 1977): 34-36.

[6] "Annual Report of Advisory Board of *Social Education*," National Council for the Social Studies, 56th Annual Meeting, November 1976.

[7] Jean Piaget, *To Understand Is To Invent* (New York: The Viking Press, Inc., 1974), p. 9.

[8] Jean Piaget, *Structuralism* (New York: Harper & Row, 1970), pp. 60-73.

[9] Hilda Taba, *Teaching Strategies and Cognitive Functioning in Elementary School Children* (San Francisco: San Francisco State College, U.S. Office of Education Cooperative Research Project No. 2404, 1966).

[10] Bruce R. Joyce, *New Strategies for Social Education* (Chicago: Science Research Associates, Inc., 1972), p. 1.

[11] Bernard Spodek, *Teaching in the Early Years* (Englewood Cliffs, New Jersey: Prentice-Hall, 1972), p. 55.

[12] Lawrence Senesh, "The Organic Curriculum: A New Experiment in Economic Education," in Joyce, *New Strategies*, pp. 117-119.

[13] John Dewey, *Experience and Education* (New York: Collier, 1963), p. 87.

[14] James P. Shaver, "A Critical View of the Social Studies Profession," *Social Education* 41:4 (April 1977): 304; and Annie L. Butler, "Today's Child—Tomorrow's World," *Young Children* 32:1 (November 1976): 4-11.

[15] Robert D. Barr, James L. Barth, and S. Samuel Shermis, *Defining the Social Studies* (Arlington, Virginia: National Council for the Social Studies, Bulletin 51, 1977), p. 52; and James P. Shaver, "A Critical View," p. 302.

[16] Barr, Barth, and Shermis, *Defining the Social Studies*, p. 61.

[17] *Ibid.*, p. 25.

[18] Helen Roberts, ed., *The Social Studies Professional* 43 (May, June 1977): 4.

[19] Arthur K. Ellis, *Teaching and Learning Elementary Social Studies* (Boston: Allyn and Bacon, Inc., 1977), p. 14.

[20] *Ibid.*, p. 104.

[21] *Ibid.*, p. 14.

[22] Jean Piaget and Barbel Inhelder, *The Psychology of the Child* (New York: Basic Books, Inc., 1969), pp. 155-156; Nathan Isaacs, *A Brief Introduction to Piaget* (New York: Agathon Press, Inc., 1972), p. 18.

[23] Butler, "Today's Child," p. 10.

[24] Alicia L. Pagano, "Learning and Creativity" (Paper delivered at the Sixth Annual Symposium of the Jean Piaget Society, Philadelphia, Pennsylvania, June 12, 1976).

[25] Morris L. Bigge, *Learning Theories for Teachers* (New York: Harper and Row, 1964), p. 14.

[26] James M. Larkin and Jane J. White, "The Learning Center in the Social Studies Classroom," *Social Education* 38:7 (November/December 1974): 689-716.

[27] John Dewey, "The Relation of Theory to Practice in Education," reprinted in Peter H. Martorella (Ed.), *Social Studies Strategies: Theory into Practice* (New York: Harper & Row Publishers, Inc., 1976), p. 4.

[28] Barr, Barth, and Shermis, *Defining the Social Studies*, p. 79.

[29] John Jarolimek, "Conceptual Approaches: Their Meaning for Elementary Social Studies," *Social Education* 30:7 (November 1966): 534-536.

[30] *Ibid.*

[31] Jerome S. Bruner, *The Process of Education* (Cambridge: Harvard University Press, 1960), p. 33.

[32] John Jarolimek, "Conceptual Approaches," p. 535.

[33] These learning activities are part of the Together We Stand Day-Care Center curriculum in Brooklyn.

[34] David Hawkins, "Messing About in Science," *Science and Children* 2:5 (February 1965).

Index

Photographs by Stanley Chu and Ellen Galinsky; Coordinator of Photography: Loren Weybright
Index by Lois Roselle
Book Design and Production by Joseph Perez
Typesetting by Byrd Press; Printing and Binding by Waverly Press